Type in Motion

2

For Liv and Em

Book design and art direction: Matt Woolman

Layout production assistance: John Stanko

First published in the United Kingdom in 2005 by
Thames & Hudson Ltd, 181A High Holborn, London WC1V 7QX

www.thamesandhudson.com

British Library Cataloguing-in-Publication Data
A catalogue record for this book is available from the British Library

ISBN-13: 978-0-500-51243-2
ISBN-10: 0-500-51243-4

342473

Printed and bound in China

Type in Motion

2

Matt Woolman

  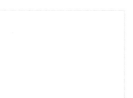 

 Thames & Hudson

Introduction   6
Back to Basics

01 Identifying   8

EyeballNYC
Off the Street   10
In the Court   12

Michael Feldman
Musical Inspiration   14
Reviving the Past   15

P2
The Space In-Between   16

Lobo
Warm and Fuzzy   18
Sublimated Beauty   20

GMUNK
Funk and Groove   22
Fast and Furious   24

FUEL
Street Smart   26

Tronic Studio
Typographic Infestation   28

Montgomery & Co. Creative
Igniting Anticipation   30
Defining the Genre   31
Top of the Food Chain   32

Stockholm Design Lab
Scandinavian Simplicity   34

Digital Kitchen
Riding the Soundwaves   36

Virginia Commonwealth University
Emotive Type   38
At Play   40

M+Motive
Drill Bits and V-Rods   42
Capturing the Moment   44

mOcean
Horror Type   46

Koo-Ki Motion Graphics
Spicing up the News   48

Trollbäck & Company
Formal Clarity   50
Reinventing the Book   51

Lebanese American University
Conceptual Type   52

02 Informing   54

Arthur Kuhn
Omniscient Type   56

Virginia Commonwealth University
Form and Counterform   58

Foreign Office
Digital Culture   62

Digital Kitchen
Protecting Creativity   64

Lebanese American University
Audiovisual Essay   66

FUEL
Teasing the Converted   68
Sweaty Serifs   69
Connecting the Dots   70

Carnegie Mellon University
History Lessons   72

04 Travelling **116**

Ten_Do_Ten
Icons in Motion 118

Fitch
Automobile Telematics 124

Guido Alvarez
Soul Hunting 126
Scenting Freedom 128

W. Bradford Paley
Literary Threads 130
Unravelling the Code 132

Yugo Nakamura
Playing with Time 134
Defying Gravity 136
Flirting with Code 138

Tronic Studio
Recalling Memory 140
Atmospheric Type 142

BüroDestruct
Architext 144

VCU – Qatar
Transformative Type 146

Kyle Barrow
Mobile Ideography 148

PIPS:lab
Graffiti in Motion 150

03 Storytelling **74**

Mirko Ilić
Intimate Characters 76
Athletic Types 78

California College of the Arts
Personal to Universal 80

Montgomery & Co. Creative
Illuminated Narratives 84
Examining the Details 86
Bar-room Banter 87

Trollbäck & Company
Capturing the Classics 88
Blind Type 90
Visual Poetry 91

InterStitch Films
Lyrical Movement 92
Ageless Elegance 93
Formal Dissection 94
Counterformal Synthesis 95

Garry Waller
Visualizing Conversation 96

Roberto de Vicq de Cumptich
& Matteo Bologna
Taming the Type 100
Type Faces 102

Foreign Office
Gestural Reality 104

Carnegie Mellon University
Story Lines 106

Digital Kitchen
Illustrating Whimsy 110

Hitoshi Takekiyo
Strictly Business 112

KeeJung Kwon
Erotica 113

John Underkoffler
Documenting Megalomania 114

05 Speculating **152**

Gicheol Lee
Typographic Organisms 154
ASCII Image 156
Bending the Rules 157

Brian Lemen
Tactile Typography 158

Chisa Yagi
Time in Motion 160

Matt Woolman
Pixel Aquarium 162

Avi Haltovsky
Scissors, Paper, Type 164

Luigi de Aloisio
Mechanical Organics 166
Simulating Nature 168

P2
Materialism 170

Reza Abedini
Persian Influence 172

Jeff Bellantoni
Alphabet City 174

Luigi de Aloisio
Clowning Around 176

Back to Basics

Type in Motion: Innovations in Digital Graphics, published in 1999, was the first book to showcase the diverse work with type and lettering in time-based media that was being produced by the many new design studios that emerged as a result of the Internet boom. Similar books followed, but not before copies found their way into the libraries of major design and film studios, advertising agencies and the hands of students and professors around the world. *Type in Motion* has been an inspiration for many, examining projects in video, film and mixed media and revealing the most cutting-edge and avant-garde talents up to 1999.

What happened next?

The dot-com bubble inflated and burst. In the fallout, a new generation of designers emerged for whom type remained the skeleton of communication. Enter *Type in Motion 2*, a chronicle of what has happened since this unprecedented period of technological advance. Many new styles have appeared, often dictated by the software of the moment. Designers are still seduced by form, but the medium is reaching maturity and there is a call for a return to basics. This does not equate to reductive aesthetics; it means beginning with a concept and building a solution from that, block by block, pixel by pixel.

The establishment of university programmes and curricula dedicated to the study of motion design has significantly contributed to this return to basics. Another key factor is access to sophisticated, yet inexpensive, software for the desktop computer. This has put much of the concept, design and production process in the hands of the professional designer and even the design student. From the development of new skills and knowledge of the entire production process comes a keen awareness of the boundless opportunities designers have.

Time-based typography is no longer a novelty with a limited application in film title sequences, it has matured into a discipline and has, in the process, become an inextricable part of branding.

Branding is the current buzz word in the design industry. Many former graphic-design firms have recast (rebranded?) themselves as branding agencies. Branding is not merely advertising, nor is it simply graphic design, rather it uses both to create a meaningful connection between company and consumer. To achieve this, designers use traditional and new communication methods, and time-based type plays a major role.

Two relatively new areas for moving typography are data-driven design and avatars. Data-driven design uses a data source to generate what is presented on screen – the animation is created by a computer algorithm rather than the designer's eye. The symbols and icons used to represent individuals, companies or organizations, have developed from inanimate objects to avatars: moving graphics that can reflect human characteristics. The increase in the variety of methods of delivering information demands that type, static logos and other visual marks adapt to specific conditions: they must act, perform and take on dynamic qualities.

The Internet, film and television industries are merging into a singular global communication network. This has lowered the barriers between geographic regions; it is common for a design studio in Brazil to do business with a client in the United States, for example. While communication technologies are increasingly global, regional and cultural influences are still evident across the various channels. It is now less about *where* one practises design than *what* one's cultural influences are.

The work in this book comes from diverse origins and has a wide array of applications, but many of the projects have an experimental aesthetic. Indeed, the pleasure of being a designer is the artistic process that one engages in, experimenting with and mastering new tools, seeking inspiration from others and playing with formal possibilities with the hope of eventually applying new visual languages to specific messages and functions in the communication sphere. It takes a risk-taking client to make this happen.

Even with advances in delivery and display technology, we are still humans with the same sensory inputs: sight, sound, touch, smell, taste. We still read in the same way, but we are slowly evolving and adapting to new conditions. For better or worse, there are those who enjoy taking the time to digest the intricacies of a *New York Times* article, while there are others who are satisfied with the visual and verbal morsels offered by *USA Today*. Many of us are somewhere in-between and are stimulated by the variety of formats and forms that type assumes. I believe the fascination and proliferation of type in motion is best summarized by the copy in the box below, which is one of many items of unknown origin passed endlessly from e-mail address to e-mail address around the world.

Another printed book on moving typography?

Type in Motion 2 picks up where *Type in Motion* left off, introducing readers to the latest work from the young and less well-known designers through to the major firms, studios and universities worldwide.

Organized around key factors for designers of type and lettering in time-based media, the book has five chapters: Identifying, Informing, Storytelling, Travelling, Speculating. Core project formats remain – computer, television, video and film – but new additions include device-based type in motion on mobile-telephone screens and automobile dashboard controls and large-scale environmental projections and displays.

Documenting a moment in time, this book is like a portable museum exhibition, an archive of what are often brief moments of success for a designer or design firm. The rapidly changing economy has not been kind to the creative industry, and many studios who enjoyed a period of success have now ceased to exist. However, the work lives on, and chronicling the continuing journey, as shown on these pages, remains important.

The paomnnehil pweor of the hmuan mnid.

Aoccdrnig to a rscheearch at Cmabrigde Uinervtisy, it deosn't mttaer in waht oredr the ltteers in a wrod are, the olny iprmoetnt tihng is taht the frist and lsat ltteer hvae to be at the rghit pclae. The rset can be a total mses and you can sitll raed it wouthit porbelm. Tihs is bcuseae the huamn mnid deos not raed ervey lteter by istlef, but the wrod as a wlohe. Amzanig huh?

The goal of branding is
to leave the audience with
an impression, creating
an identity for the product,
service or company. This
chapter considers kinetic
typography's role in the art
of branding, establishing
a meaningful connection
between the origin of the
message and its recipient.

Off the Street

EyeballNYC is a small company, based in SoHo, New York City, that specializes in graphic and type design. Producing live-action, original music and sound design and editing most of their work, they design for broadcasters, advertisers and corporations, working on everything from end-tags for X-BOX, Sprint and Duracell, to directing national advertising campaigns for Lycos, McDonald's and Trigon Blue Cross. They have created branding, promotions and show packages for companies such as Comedy Central, HBO, MTV, Bravo Networks, TV Land and Metro Channels. Another side of Eyeball's business consists of music videos and corporate work for clients like Nike, NBA Entertainment and Rawkus Records.

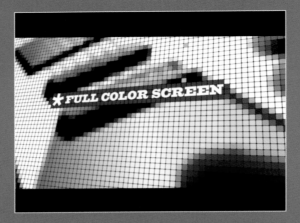

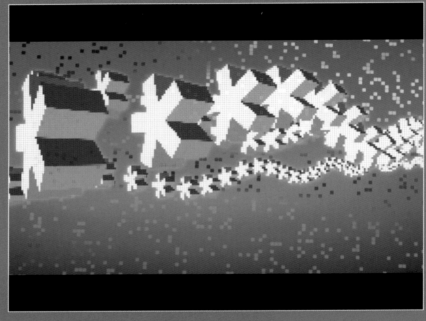

This project introduces MTV Network's first-ever branded mobile phone, dubbed the Virgin Mobile Slider V5 – MTV edition. 'Power', a thirty-second promotional film, combines MTV's brand with Virgin's sexy, sophisticated vibe and colour palette. It played over the CBS Jumbotron screen in New York and on the in-store, high-definition plasma-screen network at nationwide retail outlet Best Buy, where the Slider V5 could be purchased.

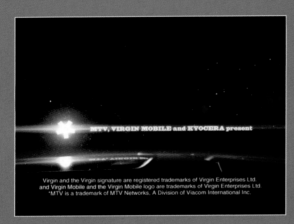

The centrepiece of the spot is a photo-real, three-dimensional model of the phone surrounded by colourful, vibrant animations that simulate the phone's colour screen and exclusive features, which include polyphonic ringtones, animated icons and one-touch access to MTV news and content. A laid-back house groove with live instrumentation and robotic vocals plays in the background. The resulting piece is funked-up, bright, full of life and in touch with MTV and Virgin's audiences.

After the original opening, each remix takes a dramatic shift, exploding in a flurry of graffiti tags and spray paint. Limore Shur, creative director of EyeballNYC, explains: 'Each transition punches you in the face and says "this is where we are now", with no subtlety about it.' Brian Sensebe, EyeballNYC's lead designer for this project, adds: 'Working on this project was a natural transition from my days as a graffiti writer. Street art is spontaneous, it just happens – I wanted to bring that same aesthetic into motion.'

TITLE POWER · FORMAT PRODUCT ID · ORIGIN USA · CLIENT MTV NETWORKS · CREATIVE DIRECTOR JULIAN BEVAN · EXECUTIVE PRODUCER MIKE EASTWOOD · EXECUTIVE PRODUCER EVE EHRICH · CG DIRECTOR STUART SIMMS · 2D ANIMATORS FABIAN TEJADA, DANNY KAMHAJI · 3D ANIMATORS VANCE MILLER, JACQUES TEGE, DAVE RINDER · EDITOR ALEX MOULTON · MUSIC EXPANSION TEAM · ARTIST SCOTT HARDKISS · MUSIC SUPERVISOR ALEX MOULTON

TITLE REMIXED · FORMAT NETWORK ID PACKAGE · ORIGIN USA · CLIENT COMEDY CENTRAL · CREATIVE DIRECTOR/VP ON-AIR DESIGN KENDRICK REID · CREATIVE DIRECTOR LIMORE SHUR · ASSOCIATE CREATIVE DIRECTOR JULIAN BEVAN · EXECUTIVE PRODUCER MIKE EASTWOOD · EXECUTIVE PRODUCER EVE EHRICH · LEAD DESIGNER/ANIMATOR BRIAN SENSEBE · 2D ANIMATORS DANNY KAMHAJI, NAOMI NISHIMURA · ORIGINAL MUSIC EXPANSION TEAM · COMPOSERS VINROC, ROGER J. MANNING JR, DJ LUX, DISCO-D, MATHEMATICS

In 2002, EyeballNYC and music company Expansion Team created a series of network identities for Comedy Central. Pleased with the results of the award-winning package and eager to entice their viewers with a sneak preview into the network's evolving look, Comedy Central challenged the companies to do it all over again. The twist was that they had to incorporate their first IDs into the new package. The results are ten 'remixed' IDs that share the same beginning as the original ones, but quickly transform into a completely new sequence, warping and twisting the visual and musical elements of the first package.

AIR ZOOM GENERATION

EyeballNYC observed that the media and various promotional campaigns had portrayed this eighteen-year-old basketball phenomenon as an incredible, larger-than-life character. They therefore created an oversized, photo-real, three-dimensional model of the Air Zoom shoe, and also manipulated images of James filmed in a large, stark white room, for the main visual elements of the spot.

Continuing a long-standing relationship with leading sports manufacturer and retailer Nike, EyeballNYC created 'Air Zoom Generation'. This sixty-second spot was to be shown on the massive video walls in Niketown stores to showcase Lebron James's first signature shoe for the brand.

Expansion Team's creative director DJ Lux and twice world-champion turntablist DJ Vinroc composed the soundtrack. By timing the visuals with the flow of the beats and scratches, sound and picture were 'remixed' into one cohesive piece.

'I approached my edits for this piece like I would one of my DJ mixes,' explained Lux, who shared editing duties. 'I'm very interested in pushing the limits of how closely picture and sound can be tied together.'

broadcast of the NBA playoffs and NBA finals, advertising agency Wieden + Kennedy New York and Brian Beletic, director for production company Smuggler, created a a four-spot TV campaign entitled '24 Seconds to Live'. They teamed-up with the Black Eyed Peas and an all-star cast of dancers, athletes and celebrities, including Carlos Santana.

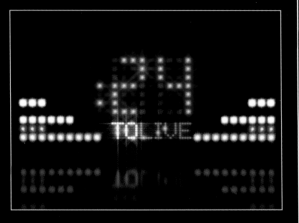

PS 260 · **SPECIAL EFFECTS** COLIN STACKPOLE @ BRANDNAME · **MUSIC** BLACK EYED PEAS FEATURING CARLOS SANTANA

ASSOCIATE CREATIVE DIRECTOR JULIAN BEVAN · **DESIGNER** DANIEL GARCIA · **EXECUTIVE PRODUCER** MIKE EASTWOOD · **PRODUCER** EVE EHRICH · **EDITOR** MAURY LOEB @

PRODUCER JESSE WANN · **PRODUCTION COMPANY** SMUGGLER · **DIRECTOR** BRIAN BELETIC · **DESIGN COMPANY** EYEBALLNYC · **CREATIVE DIRECTOR** LIMORE SHUR ·

MONTAGUE, TODD WATERBURY · **ASSOCIATE CREATIVE DIRECTOR** KEVIN PROUDFOOT/PAUL RENNER · **ART DIRECTOR** JESSE COULTER · **COPYWRITER** ILICIA WINOKUR ·

TITLE ESPN PLAYOFFS · **FORMAT** PROGRAMME ID · **ORIGIN** USA · **CLIENT** ESPN · **AGENCY** WIEDEN + KENNEDY NEW YORK · **EXECUTIVE CREATIVE DIRECTOR** TY

DIONISIO · **EXECUTIVE PRODUCER** MIKE EASTWOOD · **PRODUCER** EVE EHRICH · **LEAD DESIGNER/ANIMATOR** ADAM GAULT · **CG DIRECTOR** STUART SIMMS · **3D**

TITLE AIR ZOOM GENERATION · **FORMAT** PRODUCT ID · **ORIGIN** USA · **CLIENT** NIKE · **CREATIVE DIRECTOR** LIMORE SHUR · **ASSOCIATE CREATIVE DIRECTOR** ANDREA

ALEX MOULTON

ANIMATORS DAVE RINDER, ARVIN PALEP · **EDITOR** ALEX MOULTON · **ORIGINAL MUSIC** EXPANSION TEAM · **COMPOSERS** DJ LUX AND DJ VINROC · **MUSIC SUPERVISOR**

EyeballNYC provided additional graphic elements and type treatments to complement the theme of an elapsing shot clock that backs the Black Eyed Peas's frontman will.i.am throughout the campaign. 'Extra bling was applied to all of the graphics that we created using Trapcode's Starglow plug-in, which created a unique and organic lens flare effect', explained associate creative director, Julian Bevan. The campaign's music states the theme loud and clear: 'In this competition, there's no room to lose/so facing the opposition is what I'm gonna do/ I've got 24 seconds to live/ and 200 per cent is what I'm gonna give.' As the clock counts down from 24, the action heats up and the all-star cast joins in a musical celebration of the NBA.

Musical Inspiration

Since graduating from the graphic-design department at the University of the Arts in Philadelphia, Michael Feldman has been working as a freelance designer across a variety of mediums. His medium of choice is motion and time-based design and he has a passion for experimental music and forward-thinking design, and he is highly influenced by pop culture.

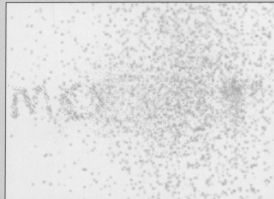

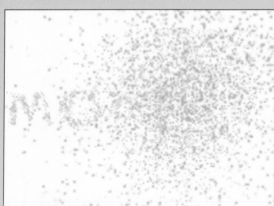

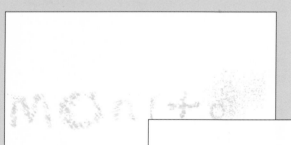

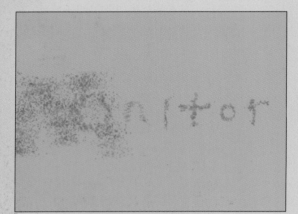

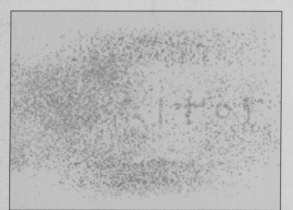

Devised for Monitor: The Dream Channel, this fifteen-second channel ID communicates the uncertainty, layering and intangibility of human dreaming. The piece's start symbolizes the opening of the eye to a dream state. The typography of the channel's logo explodes and breaks apart into fragmented colours while the highly textured, sweeping music of UK band My Bloody Valentine adds a layer of sensuality. The logo type reforms briefly, like dreams sometimes do, to unite with the tag line and identify the television channel. Finally, the typography of 'Monitor' slips and breaks apart once again falling into oblivion.

Reviving the Past

TITLE MONITOR · FORMAT NETWORK ID · ORIGIN USA · CREATIVE/
DESIGNER, PRODUCTION MICHAEL FELDMAN

TITLE MOVIES WITHIN MOVIES · FORMAT CD-ROM INTRODUCTIONS ·
ORIGIN USA · CREATIVE/DESIGNER, PRODUCTION MICHAEL FELDMAN

Connection to **Character**

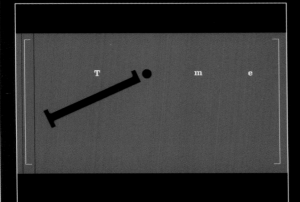

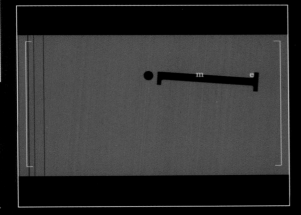

Cha | **racter**

Graphics

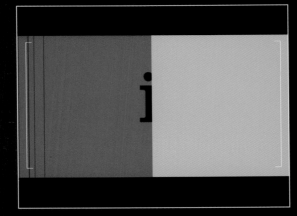

Cha /\ **acter**

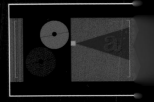

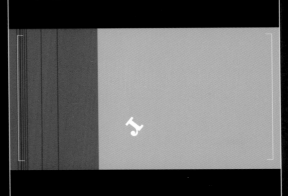

Developed as introductions
for information categories on
a CD-ROM that surveyed the
conceptual elements of film
title sequences, this montage
pays homage to classic title
sequences of the past with
a present-day design sense
and humour. With a bouncy
soundtrack, this tour-de-force
of simple animation cleverly
communicates common
themes in title sequencing
solely through the use
of typography.

The Space In-Between

The time-based commercial work of the design studio successfully blends digital technology with an assortment of more traditional materials, methods and media to produce carefully considered contemporary designs. The typography is dynamic and elegant and, although sometimes densely layered, never loses sight of its function – to communicate effectively and stimulate visually its intended audience.

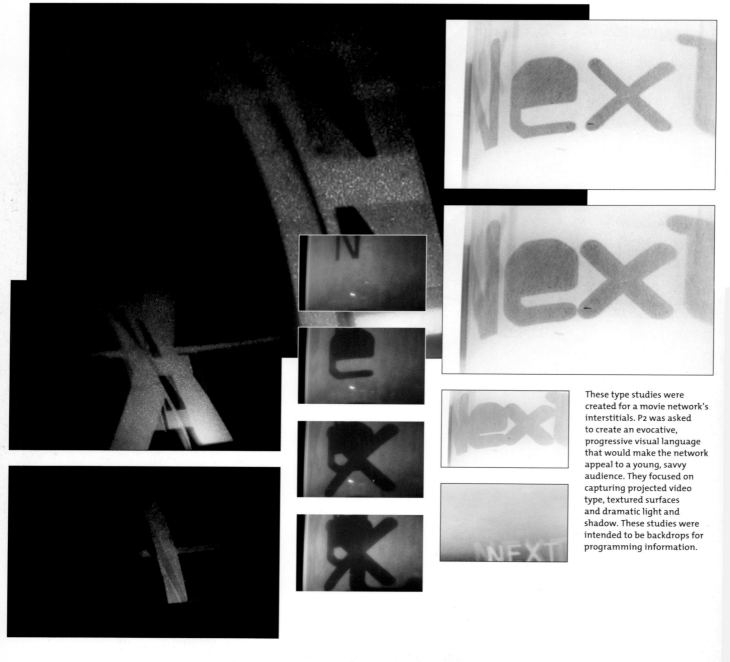

These type studies were created for a movie network's interstitials. P2 was asked to create an evocative, progressive visual language that would make the network appeal to a young, savvy audience. They focused on capturing projected video type, textured surfaces and dramatic light and shadow. These studies were intended to be backdrops for programming information.

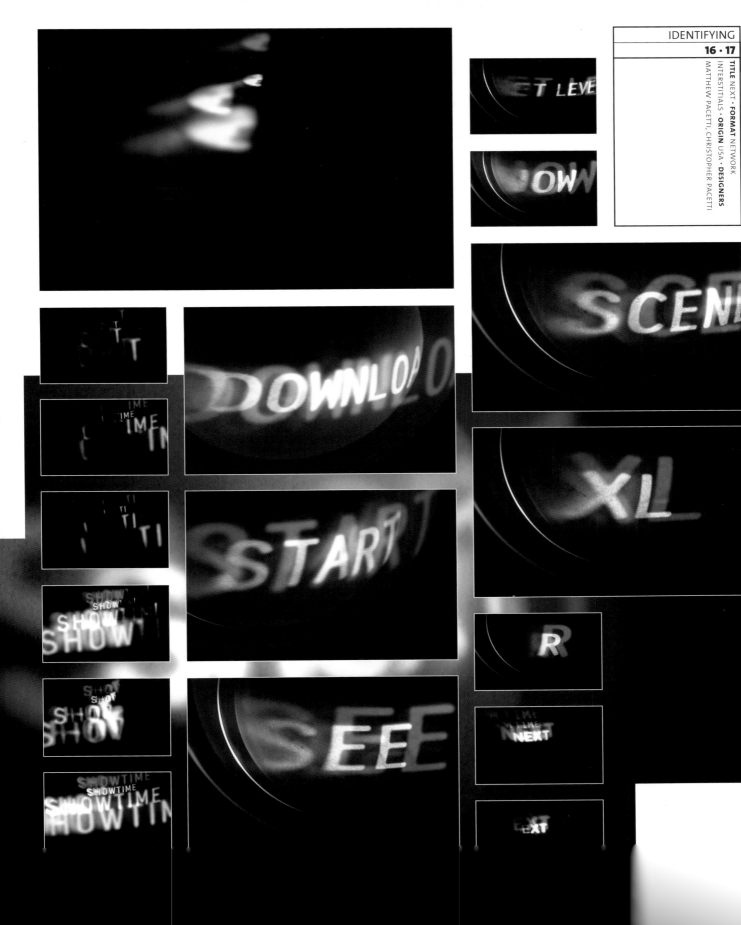

TITLE NEXT · **FORMAT** NETWORK
INTERSTITIALS · **ORIGIN** USA · **DESIGNERS**
MATTHEW PACETTI, CHRISTOPHER PACETTI

Warm and Fuzzy

Lobo is a design and animation studio based in São Paulo, Brazil. Founded in 1994, the studio has worked with major advertising agencies, television networks and the fashion industry, offering creative solutions in design, animation and effects. Lobo is recognized internationally for its contemporary design work with clients that include Ogilvy & Mather Worldwide, BBDO, McCann Erickson, MTV Brazil, Disney and Diesel.

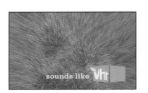

TITLE *BIG IN '02* · FORMAT PROGRAMME TEASER · ORIGIN BRAZIL · CLIENT VH1 · DESIGNER, ANIMATOR, PRODUCTION LOBO

TITLE *BIG IN '03* · FORMAT PROGRAMME TEASER · ORIGIN BRAZIL · CLIENT VH1 · DESIGNER, ANIMATOR, PRODUCTION LOBO

Every year, VH1 presents a show that is a retrospective of America's most (un)important events of the year, from pop culture to politics. Lobo was commissioned to make teasers for the show in 2002 (opposite) and 2003 (left), using a hip-hop-style soundtrack that had been provided. They transcribed each sentence of the into animated furry type for the first spot and zooming three-dimensional type for the second, both of which evoke the hyper-exaggerated, kitsch presentation of tabloid headlines.

Sublimated Beauty

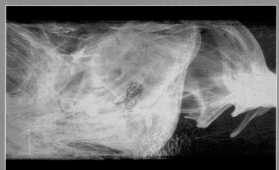

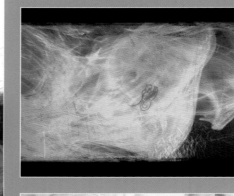

Upload is an alternative music festival in São Paulo, Brazil. Lobo created the entire graphic package for the event: flyers, website, posters and a promotional video to be shown during the festival. Basing the design on the idea that rock music is old, Lobo created graphics with an aged, antique feel.

The studio borrowed references from early-twentieth-century decoration and typography, such as Victorian and Arts and Crafts styles, and reworked them into richly layered moving collages. Playing with the type, they created textures that grow organically and change before the audience's eyes.

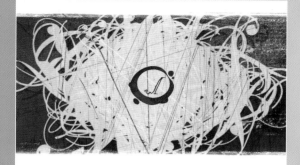

TITLE UPLOAD 2001 · **FORMAT** IDENTITY SYSTEM · **ORIGIN** BRAZIL
CLIENT FESTIVAL UPLOAD · **DESIGNER, ANIMATOR, PRODUCTION** LOBO
TITLE UPLOAD 2002 · **FORMAT** IDENTITY SYSTEM · **ORIGIN** BRAZIL
CLIENT FESTIVAL UPLOAD · **DESIGNER, ANIMATOR, PRODUCTION** LOBO

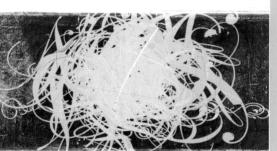

FESTIVAL UPLOAD 2002

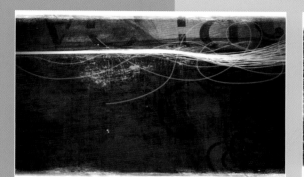

Funk and Groove

Before establishing GMUNK, a production house specializing in motion graphics, creative head Bradley Grosh had worked for numerous design companies on film, broadcast and interactive design. These included Anderson Lembke Interactive, Heavy in New York, Vir2L Studios Europe, Interactive Planet in Seattle, Imaginary Forces in Hollywood and Sydney-based Engine Design. Grosh currently freelances for various broadcast studios in Los Angeles.

MUSTANG_E_dxtr is a self-promotional piece that uses advanced Quicktime Scripting. The dancer – is it Grosh or his alter ego? – performs a series of moves for the viewer, set to a backdrop of information graphics-inspired type and forms, and the soundtrack 'I Don't Care' by DJ Dexter. The viewer can control the dancer's pace with a slide bar at the bottom of the viewing frame and a 'package cam' button calls up an inset detail shot of the dancer's assets.

This promotional piece was commissioned by the design collective We Work for Them for their DVD *Enter the Dragon*. GMUNK was given the typeface Blessed, created by We Work for Them, and was told to make a 'freestylin' piece promoting and using the typeface. GMUNK used MAYA's dynamics engine and vector render to create a study in typographical physics using three-dimensional simulations. The rapid pace of the sequence gives the viewer a dynamic experience of the typeface's kinetic and multidimensional capabilities.

TITLE MUSTANGU_E_DXTR · **FORMAT** SELF-PROMOTIONAL INTERACTIVE APPLICATION · **ORIGIN** USA · **DIRECTOR, DESIGNER** GMUNK · **PRODUCTION** DAVID GRATTON OF DONATGROUP · **SOUNDTRACK** 'I DON'T CARE', DJ DEXTER

TITLE WWFT, BAS VECTEUR · **FORMAT** PROMOTIONAL VIDEO · **ORIGIN** USA · **CLIENT** WE WORK FOR THEM · **DIRECTOR, DESIGNER, PRODUCTION, 3D ANIMATOR** GMUNK · **TYPEFACE DESIGNER** MIKE YOUNG · **SOUNDTRACK** CHAZ WINDUZ, NPFC, GMUNK

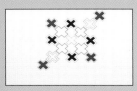

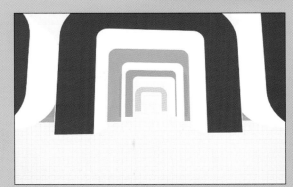

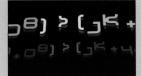

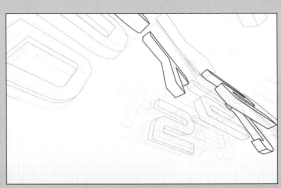

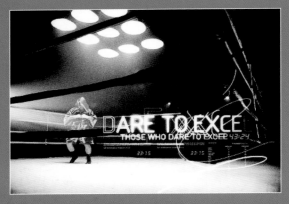

GMUNK created a dark and ominous collage of type and image to set the tone for the opening title sequence for the HBO late-night boxing special. The camera zooms in on a boxer demonstrating his moves around the ring. This is interspersed with live shots of a boxing match as provocative phrases appear. The typeface flares into a bright white light then unravels into a tangle of outlined letterforms to illustrate the explosive nature of boxing and the challenging climb to champion status.

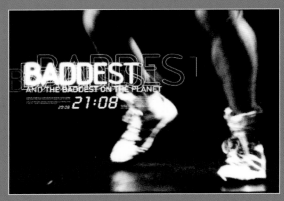

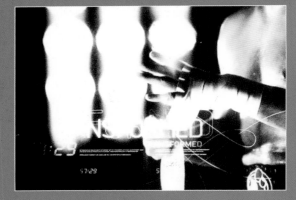

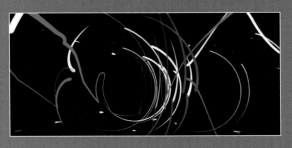

TITLE BOXING AFTER DARK · FORMAT TITLE SEQUENCE · ORIGIN USA ·
CLIENT HBO · DIRECTOR, DESIGNER, ANIMATOR, EDITOR, PRODUCTION
GMUNK · SOUNDTRACK CHAZ WINDUZ

TITLE PONTIAC VIBE · FORMAT PRODUCT PROMOTION · ORIGIN CANADA ·
CLIENT PONTIAC · AGENCY MCCANN INTERACTIVE DIRECTOR, DESIGNER,
PRODUCTION GMUNK · SOUNDTRACK CHAZ WINDUZ

Six artists were chosen
to represent a specific
characteristic of the new
Pontiac Vibe car each. GMUNK
was given *style* and decided
that a dark, expensive look
and feel to the piece would
best express this. They
extracted lines and shapes
from the contours of the car
and from the name Pontiac
Vibe, which were repeated
and interwoven in a display of
form, gesture and motion. The
piece moves from the exterior
of the car to the interior
details and finally closes with
the Vibe marque.

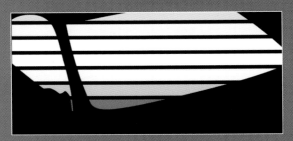

Street Smart

FUEL's designs balance energizing and innovative imagery with thoughtful and appropriate typography. The studio is known for developing inventive motion designs for clients in television, film and new media for programmes, promotions and commercial projects. FUEL's cleverly constructed animations portray a message, creating strong brand identities. Earning Emmy Award nominations and BDA and Telly Awards for recent productions have further validated FUEL's creative approach. Creative director Justin Leibow and executive producer Janet Arlotta have guided the studio's creative expansion since 2001.

FOX Corporation's Fuel television channel wanted youthful, irreverent and experimental visuals for its summer launch. Opening and closing animations were needed for an interstitial programming piece entitled

Word, which featured live-action pieces of athletes and celebrities presenting their perspectives and opinions on a variety of subjects. The design process began with mining design elements from the punk aesthetic of the 1970s and 1980s – including flyer art promoting concerts – that was raw and full of emotion. FUEL's artists worked together, drawing from the edginess of objects such as safety pins, which added a brash and daring feel.

Type treatments were also inspired by fashion designs and graphic elements, such as hand-drawn lines, paint splotches and spray-painted stencil effects. The low-tech approach was accessible with an unexpected, brazen edge. While the final designs take this low-tech approach to the point of almost appearing simplistic, there is symbolic depth to the ideas behind each of the contrasting iconic graphics and animations.

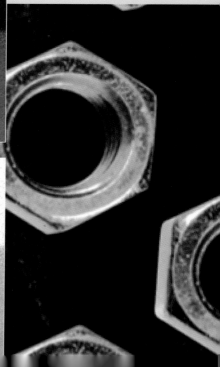

TITLE *WORD* · **FORMAT** NETWORK IDENTITY · **ORIGIN** USA · **CLIENT** FOX FUEL · **CREATIVE DIRECTOR** JUSTIN LEIBOW · **DESIGNERS, ANIMATORS** JUSTIN LEIBOW, KEVIN LAU

TITLE *VERB* · **FORMAT** PROMOTIONAL CAMPAIGN · **ORIGIN** USA · **CLIENT** CARTOON NETWORK · **CREATIVE DIRECTOR** JUSTIN LEIBOW · **DESIGNERS, ANIMATORS** JUSTIN LEIBOW, JUAN MONASTERIO

This promotional campaign was for the Cartoon Network and the government campaign 'Verb', which aimed to inspire kids to become more physically active. Promoting television programming and physical activity was an interesting juxtaposition for FUEL's designers. The typography needed to illustrate the action in a non-literal way. Their solution was to have an arrow as the main character and to animate it to express personality traits corresponding to each word.

Typographic Infestation

Tronic Studio is a directing, design and animation studio founded in the spring of 2001 in New York by Columbia architecture graduates Jesse Seppi and Vivian Rosenthal. Their work encompasses broadcast, film and experiential design, and their aim is to eliminate the delineation of one form of creative media output from another. They have delivered unique digital visions for *RES* and *Creative Review*, directed and animated spots for Nike, Fuse, MTV, the Fine Living Network and NEC, and conceived and executed projects for Diesel, GE and Wired (in-store) and Nike (online).

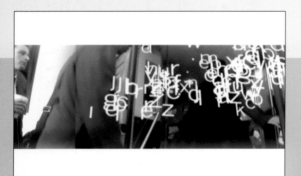

Tronic Studio brought an individual's inner voice to life in this thirty-second piece for Fine Living Network that combines live action and motion graphics.

TITLE INNER VOICE · **FORMAT** NETWORK IDENTITY · **ORIGIN** USA · **CLIENT**
LIVING NETWORK · **ANIMATOR** TRONIC STUDIO · **MUSIC** Q DEPARTMENT
TITLE PEEL · **FORMAT** NETWORK IDENTITY · **ORIGIN** USA · **CLIENT** FUSE ·
DIRECTOR, ANIMATOR TRONIC STUDIO · **MUSIC** Q DEPARTMENT
TITLE TILE · **FORMAT** NETWORK IDENTITY · **ORIGIN** USA · **CLIENT** FINE
DIRECTOR, ANIMATOR TRONIC STUDIO · **MUSIC** Q DEPARTMENT
TITLE TITLE · **FORMAT** NETWORK IDENTITY · **ORIGIN** USA · **CLIENT** FUSE ·
DIRECTOR, ANIMATOR TRONIC STUDIO · **MUSIC** Q DEPARTMENT

These network identities
for Fuse feature *Penthouse*
model Sunny Leone. In each
sequence she listens to music
on headphones with her eyes
closed while her surroundings
mutate. The word 'Fuse'
emerges from the scenery
– from bending floorboards In
'Peel' (above) and intertwining
pipes growing out of the wall
in 'Tile' (above right).

Igniting Anticipation

Based in Culver City, California, Montgomery & Co. Creative is a design firm and production company that specializes in motion design and live action for the film, television and advertising industries. George Montgomery is executive producer and creative director of the design studio, which has over twenty designers, editors, writers and producers who shape concepts into striking statements and develop all elements of the project, including image, story, sound, colour, motion and typography. The team works on numerous projects ranging from main title sequences and live-action photography to network identities.

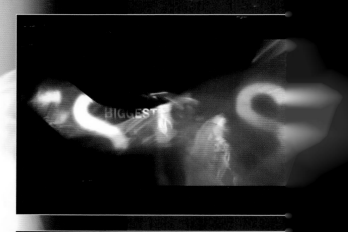

Showtime's winter Theatrical Image campaign consisted of four ninety-second advertisements. The campaign resembles movie trailers that leave viewers sitting on the edge of their seats, while providing a glimpse of the winter movie schedule.

All four trailers share the same visual elements. Footage of fire was used to convey a dynamic and explosive energy. It was composited with the words to create an organic interaction of type and texture.

The visibility of the type is determined by the images of fire, which burns and distorts it in numerous ways. Montgomery & Co. relied on multi-layered luma mattes and displacement maps, using the footage of fire as a source. Using Adobe After Effects, the type was rotoscoped to give the impression of it being 'painted' by the texture.

TITLE SHOWTIME THEATRICAL IMAGE · **FORMAT** PROGRAMME TEASER CAMPAIGN · **ORIGIN** USA · **CLIENT** SHOWTIME · **EXECUTIVE CREATIVE DIRECTOR** GEORGE MONTGOMERY · **DESIGNER** MONTGOMERY & CO. CREATIVE

TITLE HBO GENRE OPEN · **FORMAT** OPENING SEQUENCES · **ORIGIN** USA **CLIENT** HBO · **EXECUTIVE CREATIVE DIRECTOR** GEORGE MONTGOMERY **DESIGNER** MONTGOMERY & CO. CREATIVE

These graphic sequences are for HBO's original programme genres: Original Series, Original Movie, Comedy, Sports, Documentaries, Late Night, Music Events, Mini Series and Special Presentations. The motion graphics and typography for the nine individual pieces have distinct animations and colour palettes designed to reflect the mood of each genre. Each piece begins with the typography on the horizon, from where it progresses to behind the camera, giving the piece maximum depth. As the typography moves along an extreme horizontal axis, each letter is animated individually giving it a highly kinetic feel. The type flows smoothly and constantly throughout the piece as each word is revealed.

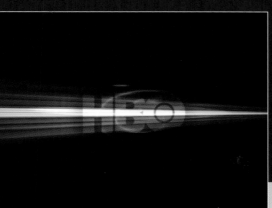

Top of the Food Chain

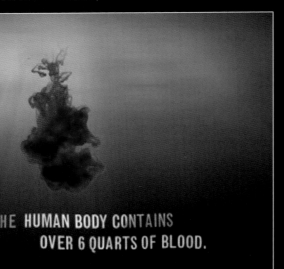

THE **HUMAN BODY** CONTAINS
OVER 6 QUARTS OF BLOOD.

A SHARK CAN SNIFF
OUT A SINGLE DROP...

FROM A QUARTER MILE AWAY

Part of the promotional campaign for Discovery Channel's Shark Week, Montgomery & Co. aimed to create each sequence from the shark's point of view. They rented a large water tank and used an underwater camera crew to capture footage. In addition, a green-screen was placed behind the large glass tank so that they could add a wavelike, watery background.

'Blood Drop' focuses on a drop of blood in the water, which disperses and grows larger until it suddenly retracts into one tight drop and then morphs into the Shark Week logo. Montgomery & Co. experimented with several liquids to replicate the look of real blood. Once the shots were graphically treated, sound design and music were added to enhance the sense of fear in this piece.

WATCHING YOU

YOU *JUST* SWIM IN IT

FOREVER

SHARK WEEK

COMING IN JULY

MY WORLD

TITLE SHARK WEEK, 'BLOOD DROP' · FORMAT PROGRAMME PROMOTION ORIGIN USA · CLIENT DISCOVERY CHANNEL · EXECUTIVE CREATIVE DIRECTOR GEORGE MONTGOMERY · DIRECTOR OF PHOTOGRAPHY PETER ROMANO · DESIGNER MONTGOMERY & CO. CREATIVE

TITLE SHARK WEEK, 'SWIMMER' · FORMAT PROGRAMME PROMOTION ORIGIN USA · CLIENT DISCOVERY CHANNEL · EXECUTIVE CREATIVE DIRECTOR GEORGE MONTGOMERY · DIRECTOR OF PHOTOGRAPHY PETER ROMANO · DESIGNER MONTGOMERY & CO. CREATIVE

The sequences appear to have been filmed in nature, but never actually show a shark. Yet all of them, including 'Swimmer' (shown), are infused with intense energy and emotion, immersing the viewers in the unknown terrors of the deep.

Discovery

CHANNEL

entertain your brain

Scandinavian Simplicity

Founded in 1998 by architect Thomas Eriksson, art director Björn Kusoffsky and design strategist Göran Lagerström, Stockholm Design Lab is a multidisciplinary design company that operates internationally. Their goal is to create high-quality design that makes a difference; the studio maintains a design philosophy rooted in Scandinavia and based on the fundamental ideas of simplicity, innovation and excellence. Projects range from comprehensive identity campaigns, packaging programmes, retail and corporate environments to title sequences and books.

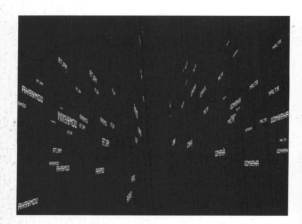

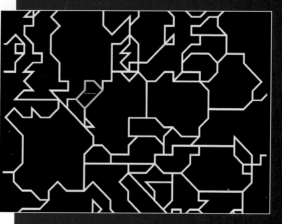

This promotional sequence for the Eurovision Song Contest Stockholm 2000, seen by more than 100 million viewers worldwide, features live-action footage of travellers, transportation and poetic, natural environments, interspersed with names of international cities and participating countries.

TITLE EUROVISION SONG CONTEST 2000 · **FORMAT** PROGRAMME IDENTITY · **ORIGIN** SWEDEN · **CLIENT** SVERIGES TELEVISION · **CREATIVE DIRECTOR, DESIGNER, PRODUCTION** STOCKHOLM DESIGN LAB

TITLE *STUDIO POP* · **FORMAT** PROGRAMME TITLE SEQUENCE · **ORIGIN** SWEDEN · **CLIENT** SVERIGES TELEVISION · **CREATIVE DIRECTOR, DESIGNER, PRODUCTION** STOCKHOLM DESIGN LAB

Doves fly in slow motion within a large empty interior space as a labyrinth of lines form letters that spell the title *Studio Pop*. The programme appears on Sveriges Television, Sweden's public service network.

Riding the Soundwaves

With offices in Seattle and Chicago, Digital Kitchen has been at the centre of contemporary design, film-making and visual culture for over fifteen years. The creative environment at Digital Kitchen reflects those found in advertising agencies, yet it does not limit itself to traditional advertising models. Employing musicians, artists, film-makers and classically trained designers, Digital Kitchen draws from a much broader creative palette than traditional design, marketing and production firms. Digital Kitchen considers motion design the pre-eminent tool in creating brand identities in the twenty-first century.

Digital Kitchen created a series of identity sequences for the Experience Music Project, a unique museum that combines interactive and interpretive exhibits to tell the story of American popular music.

Each sequence combines music with visual elements to illustrate the spontaneous, passionate and unique pathways of creative expression in its various forms: jazz, classic rock, hip-hop, electronic and so on.

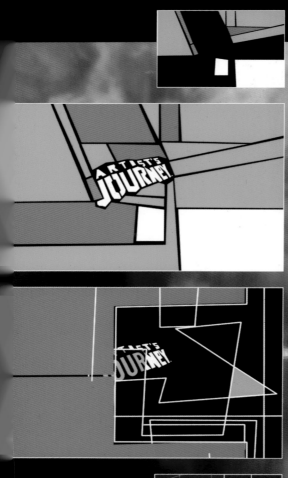

Evolution traces the development of music through significant stylistic benchmarks – visual and sonic – and is centred around the 'Artist's Journey' logo. The journey begins with an intricate collage of cut shapes that assemble to a jazz soundtrack, conjuring up the pinnacle of the 1950s jazz era. The space between the shapes transforms into a network of lines that mutates into electrical soundwaves, signifying the move into the 1960s rock generation. Slowly the electrified lines swirl into the psychedelic backdrop of late-1960s San Francisco rock.

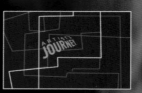

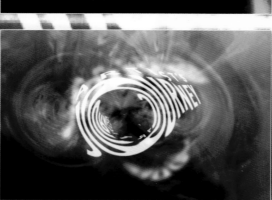

TITLE EXPERIENCE MUSIC PROJECT, EVOLUTION • **FORMAT** IDENTITY SEQUENCE • **ORIGIN** USA • **CLIENT** VULCAN VENTURES • **PRODUCTION, DESIGNER, DIRECTOR, MOTION GRAPHICS, EDITOR** DIGITAL KITCHEN

The electric 1960s gives way to the electronic 1970s and 1980s as cathode-ray patterns emerge. Pop, hip-hop and other styles merge together as the sequence draws to a close with the tag 'ride the music'.

Emotive Type

Students on the interaction design course taught by Sandy Wheeler in the communication design course, School of the Arts, Virginia Commonwealth University were challenged to create a ten-second (120-frame) typographic narrative with sound. Using the letters of a single word or the complete alphabet, the narrative had to have an emotive quality. Students were also asked to consider typographic contrast, storyboarding, time, contrasts in motion, sequential movement, transitions and sound.

The viewer of this animation becomes the audience of a comedian's performance. Set in the typeface Futura Extra Black, this comedian is not drawing laughs, but boos. As the letters of the word gyrate to a muffled delivery, red 'a's emerge from the foreground, resembling eggs being thrown at the struggling performer. As the letters splat against the word, the black letters become red in embarrassment, until the entire word is left on stage in silence.

TITLE COMEDIAN · **FORMAT** DIGITAL ANIMATION · **ORIGIN** USA · **INSTRUCTOR** SANDY WHEELER · **DESIGNER, ANIMATOR** CAROLYN BELEFSKI

TITLE CLONE · **FORMAT** DIGITAL ANIMATION · **ORIGIN** USA · **INSTRUCTOR** SANDY WHEELER · **DESIGNER, ANIMATOR** GRIER DILL

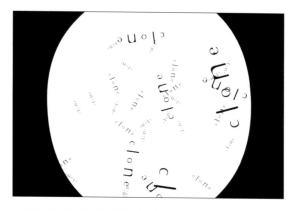

clone

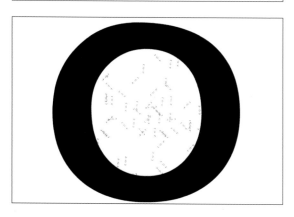

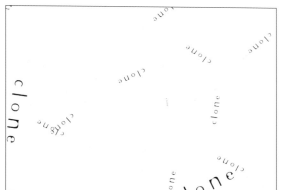

Cl one

one

This animation begins with the word 'clone' placed off-centre. As the image focuses in on the letter 'o', tiny floating particles appear in its counterform, which slowly emerge as the word 'clone' repeated over and over. Before long, the viewer is swimming in clones. One of the words then uprights itself, moves to the centre of the screen and drops its 'cl', leaving the word 'one' by itself.

This animation brings together on screen two capital Gs – one in the typeface Ultra Bodoni and the other in Futura sans serif. The Bodoni character appears first, then the Futura slides in from the left and moves in front of the heavier letterform. A cyan dot begins to roll around the space formed by the overlapping letters in a playful circuit, while the two Gs rotate in opposite directions, but on the same axis. The dot eventually falls out of the shape created by the combined letterforms and the Gs return to their original state.

TITLE GS AND A DOT · **FORMAT** DIGITAL
ANIMATION · **ORIGIN** USA · **INSTRUCTOR**
SANDY WHEELER · **DESIGNER, ANIMATOR**
BRYAN KEPLESKY

TITLE ALPHABET · **FORMAT** DIGITAL
ANIMATION · **ORIGIN** USA · **INSTRUCTOR**
SANDY WHEELER · **DESIGNER, ANIMATOR**
EVAN COTTER

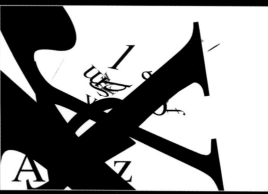

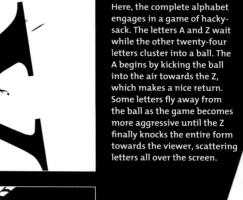

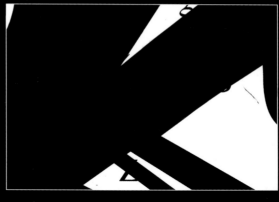

Here, the complete alphabet engages in a game of hacky-sack. The letters A and Z wait while the other twenty-four letters cluster into a ball. The A begins by kicking the ball into the air towards the Z, which makes a nice return. Some letters fly away from the ball as the game becomes more aggressive until the Z finally knocks the entire form towards the viewer, scattering letters all over the screen.

Drill Bits and V-Rods

In 2000, design firms M, Inc., led by creative director and principal Joel Markus, and Motive, headed by director Robert Hoffman, partnered up to form M+Motive. The resulting multidisciplinary design and effects consortium specializes in creative direction, design and production for regional, national and international clients. The team has garnered widespread recognition for its designs for The Learning Channel, Discovery Channel USA and International, Home and Garden Channel, ESPN International and for regional television networks.

The television programme *Monster House* is as much about ripping a house apart as renovating it in a specific style, and M+Motive wanted the campaign to reflect this. The sequence begins with a sheet of paper showing a week on a calendar. A drill bit rips through the paper, uncovering the title and broadcast date of a specific episode, then stops spinning to reveal the *Monster House* logo. M+Motive designed the logo and built it as a physical prop that they filmed spinning from several angles and distances.

Harley Davidson: Birth of the V-Rod is a documentary about the design and manufacture of the V-Rod's sleek, aluminium, liquid-cooled engine. M+Motive's inspiration for the title design came from the existing Harley Davidson colour palette: black, orange and white. They used a limited number of visual elements, creating a typographically driven motion title sequence. M+Motive wanted to emulate the V-Rod engine's initial start up; abstract elements of the cycle were introduced to complement the typography.

IDENTIFYING

42 · 43

TITLE MONSTER HOUSE WEEK · **FORMAT** PROGRAMME IDENTITY · **ORIGIN** USA · **CLIENT** DISCOVERY CHANNEL: MARY CLARE BAGUET, JEFF STRONG, PATRICIA TONG · **DESIGN DIRECTOR** JOEL MARKUS (M, INC.) · **DESIGNER** ROBERT HOFFMAN (MOTIVE) · **PRODUCTION** M+MOTIVE

TITLE HARLEY DAVIDSON: BIRTH OF THE V-ROD · **FORMAT** PROGRAMME IDENTITY · **ORIGIN** USA · **CLIENT** DISCOVERY CHANNEL: DAN STANTON, JEFF STRONG · **DESIGN DIRECTOR** JOEL MARKUS (M, INC.) · **DESIGNERS** ROBERT HOFFMAN (MOTIVE), JOEL MARKUS (M, INC.) · **PRODUCTION** M+MOTIVE

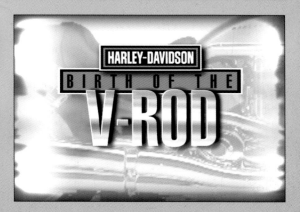

Capturing the Moment

Broadcast in Latin America, this five-second introduction for commercial sponsors to present a sports moment on ESPN needed to be in three languages: Spanish, Portuguese and English. M+Motive designed an animated typographic texture composed of the word 'moment' in all three languages. The words were filled with sports footage and graphics, resulting in a very fast and energetically paced sequence as the sports scenes are revealed through the strokes of richly layered letterforms.

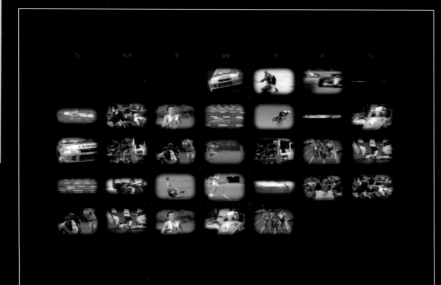

M+Motive designed a package of sequences to promote ESPN's weekly schedule internationally, including opening and closing sequences, spots for each day of the week, transitions and the ESPN logo, all in English, Spanish and Portuguese. M+Motive's created an animated calendar on which the days of the week serve as mini television monitors flickering on and off, displaying all the sports events on the schedule. The days and titles animate in front of the monitors at a faster pace creating a visual rhythm between the typography and monitors.

TITLE MOMENTS ON ESPN · FORMAT NETWORK IDENTITY · ORIGIN USA · CLIENT ESPN INTERNATIONAL: ANDY BRONSTEIN, ALBERT FELIX COLON · DESIGN DIRECTOR JOEL MARKUS (M, INC.) · DESIGNER ROBERT HOFFMAN (MOTIVE) · PRODUCTION M+MOTIVE

TITLE WHAT'S ON ESPN THIS WEEK · FORMAT NETWORK IDENTITY · ORIGIN USA · CLIENT ESPN INTERNATIONAL: ANDY BRONSTEIN, ALFREDO CÓRDOBA · DESIGN DIRECTOR JOEL MARKUS (M, INC.) · DESIGNER JOEL MARKUS (M, INC.) · DESIGNER, ANIMATOR FRANÇOIS BERELOWITCH · PRODUCTION M, INC.

Horror Type

California-based mOcean is a creative marketing agency that produces campaigns for film, television, the Internet and print. Its multicultural team – representing Argentina, Cuba, Brazil, Korea, Colombia, Germany, Canada and the United States – means that each individual brings a unique perspective to mOcean's collaborative style of work, creating a fresh, imaginative approach to their projects both in motion graphics and editorial content.

This award-winning identity package is based on horror-film posters of the 1950s. The sequences begin in two-dimensional space with a deceptively serene landscape, such as a metropolitan skyline, and a contextual tag, 'Target Earth' for example, set in a classic horror-film typeface. The scene slowly animates to reveal a three-dimensional depth as the posters come alive with action and dramatic phrases such as 'Spine-Tingling Experience'. The closing scene settles on the series title, *Monsters HD*. While each sequence is based on a different classic horror-film genre – sea monsters, aliens, slashers, Godzilla, vampires, ghosts, robots, the undead – a tightly designed system is evident when the title designs are placed together (opposite).

TITLE *MONSTERS HD* · FORMAT NETWORK IDENTITY PACKAGE · ORIGIN USA · CLIENT VOOMI NETWORK/RAINBOW MEDIA · EXECUTIVE PRODUCER TERESA ANTISTA · CREATIVE DIRECTOR STEVE KAZANJIAN · 2D DESIGNERS/ ANIMATORS DAVID PAGANI, SUZI ZIMMERMANN · 3D DESIGNERS/ ANIMATORS MIKE NAVARRO, SHANE ZUCKER · COMPOSER ROB CAIRNS · SOUND DESIGN EFFECTS/MIXER WILLIE LEVINS

Spicing up the News

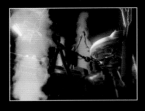

Koo-Ki Motion Graphics is a screen-media production company based in Japan, which has planned and directed a diverse range of motion-design projects, including television commercials, computer-generated works and broadcast motion graphics. Exploring distinctive concepts in every project, the studio has an idiosyncratic creative style.

Koo-Ki designed a range of title sequences for the music channel Vibe. The first, *What's Cool*, is for an information programme on cool topics. A close-up tour of scientific instruments establishes a laboratory scene. It ends on a petri dish in which a bacteria experiment has grown to form the logo for the programme. The thriving culture continues to grow until it completely obscures the letterforms.

The second sequence, *What's Hot*, identifies a programme delivering the hottest news. Koo-Ki created a factory of automated robots assembling a series of programme logos from molten metal.

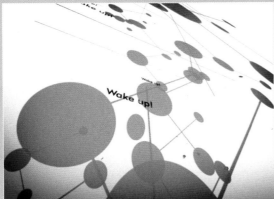

TITLE WHAT'S COOL, WHAT'S HOT · **FORMAT** PROGRAMME OPENING
IDENTITIES · **ORIGIN** JAPAN · **CLIENT** VIBE TELEVISION · **DIRECTOR,**
DESIGNER, PRODUCTION KOO-KI MOTION GRAPHICS

TITLE WAKE UP! · **FORMAT** PROGRAMME OPENING IDENTITY ·
ORIGIN JAPAN · **CLIENT** YOMIURI TELECASTING CORP. · **PRODUCER**
KAZUMUNE YAMAMOTO · **DIRECTOR** MOTOHIRO SHIRAKAWA ·
AUDIO YOSHIFUMI ASA

For this morning news programme, Koo-Ki wanted to portray making a fresh start to the day, and to create an upbeat, accessible image for what can be an overwhelming array of news events. They produced a complex information web to illustrate the many stories of the day, but instead of making it complicated and ominous, they integrated bright colours and movement. The viewer flies through the web as the sterile geometric typeface spelling 'Wake up!' breaks away into colourful confetti, revealing a stylized, classic, serif typeface that eases the viewer into the show.

you know and applying it to new areas so as
a company and as individuals, you can grow
creatively.' The firm's diverse creative output
includes commercials, film titles, environmental
installations and network television branding
as well as magazines, T-shirts and snowboard
graphics. Known throughout television, film and
design industries for its clean aesthetic and avant-
garde approach, the company has rapidly risen
to prominence. Through little more than word-
of-mouth, the three-year-old firm has attracted
a diverse mix of design projects for clients that
include HBO, TNT, AMC, Sundance Channel, Volvo
and Sony.

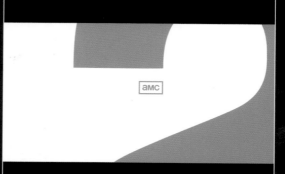

To reinvent the AMC network,
Trollbäck & Company turned
to American films' most
important component: the
fans. Creating the tag line, 'TV
For Movie People', Trollbäck
& Company designed and
produced a highly successful
brand identity that centres
on real fans attempting
to explain their love of
favourite films in the
passionate, insightful and
amusing manner only cinema
zealots can.

'We wanted to get to the core
of what this community of
American film fans love about
film without being nostalgic,'
said the project's creative
director Joe Wright. 'Rather
than using flashy three-
dimensional graphics with
layered lens flares, we decided
to use people on a white
background talking honestly
to the camera about why they
love film.'

TITLE AMC NETWORK BRANDING · **FORMAT** NETWORK BRANDING
CAMPAIGN · **ORIGIN** USA · **CLIENT** AMC NETWORK · **DIRECTOR** JAKOB
TROLLBÄCK · **CREATIVE DIRECTORS** JOE WRIGHT, GREG HAHN · **EDITORS**
NICOLE AMATO, STEPHEN CHEIFITZ · **MUSIC** SACRED NOISE

TITLE VISIONS REALIZED · **FORMAT** IMAGE SPOT · **ORIGIN** USA · **CLIENT** HBO
FILMS · **CREATIVE DIRECTOR** ANTOINE TINGUELY · **PRODUCER** ELIZABETH
KIEHNER · **EDITOR** NICOLE AMATO · **COMPUTER GRAPHICS ARTIST**
CHRIS HAAK

Reinventing the Book

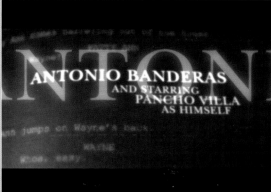

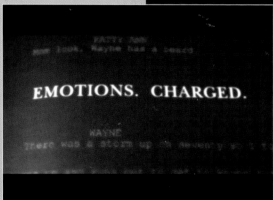

Pages from film scripts are
used as a graphic device for
the titles in this sequence,
which communicates HBO
Films' commitment to
high-quality writing and
storytelling. Actual pages
were shot to create a range
of effects. Later the page
turns were re-created
using computer-generated
animation so that Trollbäck &
Company could have greater
flexibility to adjust copy.

Conceptual Type

These projects come from the advanced typography course taught by Yasmine Taan at the Lebanese American University in Beirut, Lebanon. The students were asked to design an Arabic typeface based on a concept of their choice, then create an animation to promote it.

Dana Sayed's Arabic typeface is called *Fakakeeh*, meaning 'blown-up stuff' or 'bubbles'. Sayed did not rely on a basic shape when designing the font, but used a horizontal straight line that the letterforms are either stuck to, hung from by a thread or connected to in some way. When the letters are not connected, the straight line ends and a new one begins.

Sayed applied both the positive letters and the spaces created from reversed-out lettering. 'In designing my letters I relied on the visual aspect to let my letters breathe in terms of positive and negative space and on the concept of attachment to the straight line.'

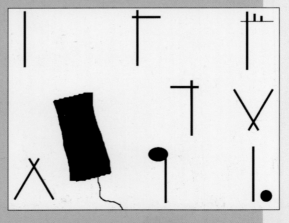

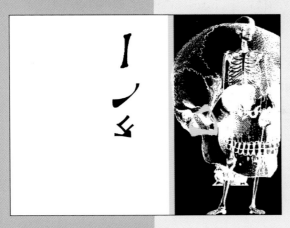

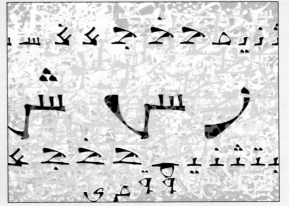

TITLE FAKAKEH · **FORMAT** TYPEFACE/TYPEFACE ANIMATION · **ORIGIN** LEBANON · **FACULTY ADVISOR** YASMINE TAAN · **DESIGNER,** **PRODUCTION** DANA SAYED

TITLE AL MALOUNE · **FORMAT** TYPEFACE/TYPEFACE ANIMATION · **ORIGIN** LEBANON · **FACULTY ADVISOR** YASMINE TAAN · **DESIGNER,** **PRODUCTION** HATEM HAMOUI

Al Maloune ('the damned') is an Arabic typeface created from modules based on shapes from the human skeleton. The character structure is divided into four primary parts and one secondary part: one ascender, two body heights and two descenders. The letter sizes are in proportion to each other and carefully designed to be legible and to avoid clashing when the size is reduced.

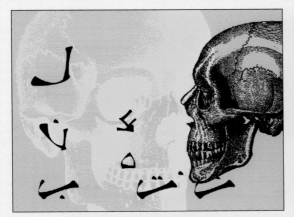

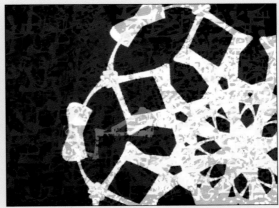

The examples considered
in this chapter deliver
information about a product,
service or event. The medium
– type and lettering – creates
a message, which may be
supported by image and
sound.

Omniscient Type

Networked Literature: The Parables of Jesus
is a project created by Arthur Kuhn for his
undergraduate work in the Digital Design Program
at the University of Cincinnati. The impetus
for this project was to explore new types of
interaction beyond the dominant 'text on page'
manipulated by a keyboard and mouse. Exploring
new approaches reveals how they can change the
way we interact with text, so that reading returns
to its ancient roots and becomes a collective,
participatory experience. These projects also
provide ways to better understand the communal
and cultural context in which the text was written.

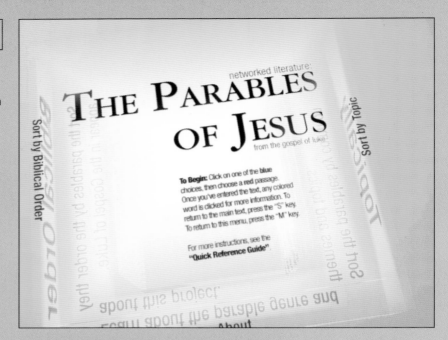

Kuhn writes: 'Today the Bible,
and many other works of
antiquity, has lost much. The
text may have been preserved,
but the context in which that
text was intended to exist has
disappeared. This context will
continue to degrade more and
more in the future. However,
using technology we can
reverse this trend. We can
render cultural context and
the context of community.
Perhaps this trend can be
reversed and the rich sense
of depth and milieu can be
returned to literature.'

Kuhn created this highly
interactive and information-
dense three-dimensional
world where text, notes
on cultural context, cross-
references and commentary
exist in the same space. The
space and interactivity are
created using LINGO – the
programming language for
the application Macromedia
Director 3D. The digital
environment is navigated
using an interface structure
that is essentially transparent.

TITLE NETWORKED LITERATURE: THE PARABLES OF JESUS · **FORMAT** DIGITAL INTERACTIVE APPLICATION · **ORIGIN** USA · **DESIGNER, PROGRAMMER** ARTHUR KUHN

Colour codes indicate clickable areas to obtain more information. Red words enable the reader to interact with the main menu or to review commentary on a selected passage. Green words reveal definitions of words or phrases, or allow the reader to review culturally relevant information.

Good Samaritan

Luke 10:25-37

The Servant's Role

"A man was going down from [Jerusalem to Jericho], when he fell into the hands of [robbers], when they stripped him of his clothes, beat him and went away, leaving him half dead. A priest happened to be going down the same road, and when he saw the man, he passed by on the other side. So too, a Levite, when he came to the place and saw him, passed by on the other side. But a Samaritan, as he traveled, came where the man was; and when he saw him, he took pity on him. He went to him and bandaged his wounds, pouring on oil..."

Jerusalem - The capital city of the nation of Israel. It was the cultural, spiritual and economic head of the Jewish people. The city was home to the most important complex in the 1st Century Jewish world, the Temple.

Jericho - By the first century, Jericho was occupied the Romans. By the first century, Jericho was rebuilt by Herod the Great as a resort city.

Jerusalem to Jericho - A 17-mile road. This trip was often made through the century merchants. It was also known for being fairly dangerous, a feeding ground for /lego/ (translated as bandits).

Levite - Descendants...

Biblical Order

Sort the parables by the order they appear in the Gospel of Luke.

...insolvent, but one of them owed him, ten times more than the... *em both*, and did not take the advantage of the law against them, ...ildren to be sold, or *deliver them to the tormentors*. Now they were ...eived; but *which of them will love him most?* ...*gave most*; and herein he rightly judged. Now we, ... be *forgiven*, may hence learn the duty between

...ght to make satisfaction to his creditor. No man can ...table enjoyment of it, but that which is so when all

...e debtor to pay his debt, the creditor ought not to be ...our of the law with him, but freely to forgive him. ...stretched into rigour becomes unjust. Let the ...uria--*The law stretched into rigour becomes unjust*. Let the ...t parable, Matt. xviii. 23, &c., and tremble; for they shall have ...t show no mercy.

...d his creditors merciful ought to be very grateful to them; and, if he ...them, ought to love them. Some insolvent debtors, instead of ...se them, ought to love them. to their creditors that lose by them, and cannot give them a good ...whereas losers may have leave to speak. But this parable ...himself, for he it is that forgives, and is ...here [1.] That sin is a

Form and Counterform

Animation is becoming increasingly prevalent in interaction design as a means to enliven and enrich simple navigational elements or as a way to deliver primary content. These projects were produced on the interaction design course taught by Roy McKelvey in the Communication Design Program, School of the Arts, Virginia Commonwealth University.

For this project, students focused on the use of animation as an explanatory device, while also learning to use Macromedia Flash. Their challenge was to create a thirty-second animation to demonstrate the essential features and unique characteristics of a given typeface or font in an informative and entertaining way. Caslon and Lubalin Graph were used in these two examples.

Cas

Caslon

Casl   1725

ABCDEFG
HIJKLMN
OPQRSTU
VWXYZ

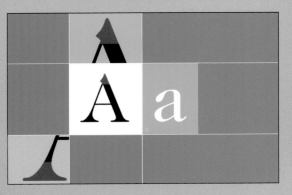

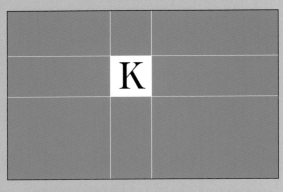

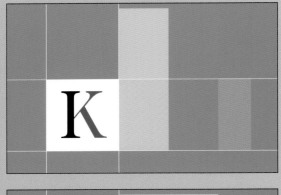

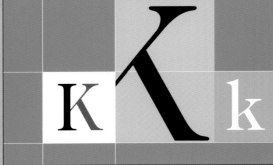

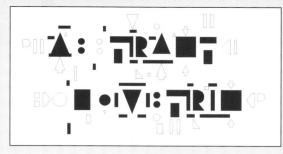

TITLE CASLON · **FORMAT** DIGITAL
ANIMATION · **ORIGIN** USA · **INSTRUCTOR**
ROY MCKELVEY · **DESIGNER, ANIMATOR**
ANITA ERADLA

TITLE LUBALIN GRAPH · **FORMAT** DIGITAL
ANIMATION · **ORIGIN** USA · **INSTRUCTOR**
ROY MCKELVEY · **DESIGNER, ANIMATOR**
JOSH RHETT

In planning their animation, students must determine the balance of praxis and poetics in the piece. That is, they must decide whether to emphasize the fixed categorizations of typographic scholars, or to take a more organic approach to revealing the typeface's features. There may be significant overlap in the details of letterforms shown in each approach, but the attitude of the presentations vary significantly.

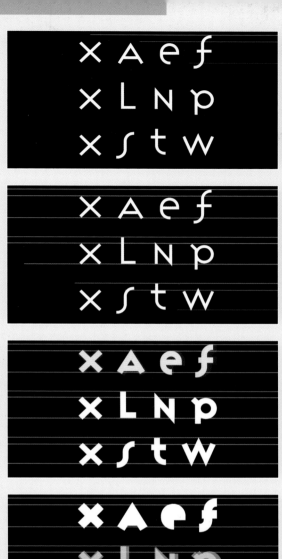

INFORMING

60 · 61

TITLE ARIAL NARROW · **FORMAT** DIGITAL
ANIMATION · **ORIGIN** USA · **INSTRUCTOR**
ROY MCKELVEY · **DESIGNER, ANIMATOR**
PAUL CANTOR

TITLE VARIEX · **FORMAT** DIGITAL ANIMATION ·
ORIGIN USA · **INSTRUCTOR** ROY MCKELVEY ·
DESIGNER, ANIMATOR JASON POULOS

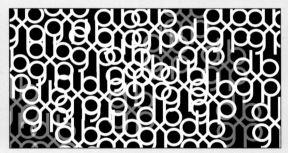

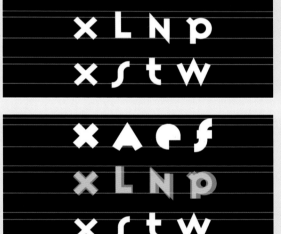

Digital Culture

Started when founding partners Sonia Ortiz Alcon, Matteo Manzini and Fredrik Nordbeck met while studying graphic design at Central Saint Martins College of Art and Design, Foreign Office is a directing and design studio based in London. They have cultivated a wide range of interests and talents, including graphics, web design, animation and film-making, which is currently their main focus. They borrow freely from all their skills, styles and experience to best suit their clients' communication needs.

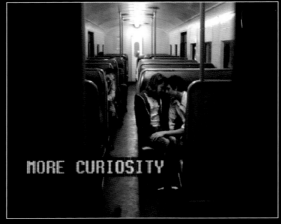

The advertisement for Czech telecommunications company Eurotel aimed to convey the message that personal lives can be improved through better telecommunication. Foreign Office's idea was to use a very personal, intimate medium and so borrowed the type style and animation of mobile-phone text messaging. The way the letters appear mimics the 'predictive text' function of mobile phones, a very familiar sight for millions of 'texting' addicts around the world.

WHAT ARE YOU WAITING FOR?

MORE STAGES?

MORE BEATS?

MORE GROUPIES?

MORE GUITARS?

MORE ACTION?

TITLE MORE LIFE · FORMAT PRODUCT PROMOTION · ORIGIN CZECH REPUBLIC ·
CLIENT EUROTEL · AGENCY LEO BURNETT PRAGUE · DIRECTOR STEVE GREEN ·
PRODUCER PAVLA BURGETOVA · PRODUCTION COMPANY STILLKING FILMS ·
DESIGNER, ANIMATOR FOREIGN OFFICE

TITLE MORE MUSIC · FORMAT PRODUCT PROMOTION · ORIGIN UK · CLIENT
COCA-COLA COMPANY · AGENCY SPRINGER JACOBY HAMBURG · DIRECTORS
BRIAN BELETIC, BEN MOR · PRODUCERS DANIEL BERGMANN, BRIAN CARMODY ·
PRODUCTION COMPANY STINK/SMUGGLER · TYPEFACE DESIGNER, ANIMATOR
FOREIGN OFFICE

Coca-Cola asked Foreign Office to produce a modern, dynamic type treatment and animation that conveyed their brand message. Images of people break up in a grid of electronic-looking squares on a black background while a 'fizzy' animation reveals the type superimposed on the image, using the same square grid. The square-based typeface was inspired by LED boards that display sports results. The square gauge was critical since the campaigns went out in many languages and some words were very long.

Protecting Creativity

Digital Kitchen (see p. 36) was asked by Artists Against Piracy to create a series of public-service announcements as part of their campaign to help artists defend the copyright on their work. The sequences were centred on the copyright symbol, which communicates law and business – two things that inspire hostility from core music consumers, according to Digital Kitchen's executive creative director Paul Matthaeus.

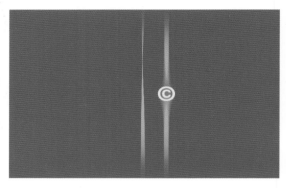

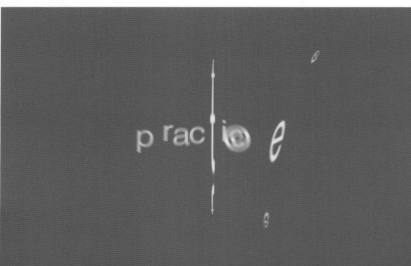

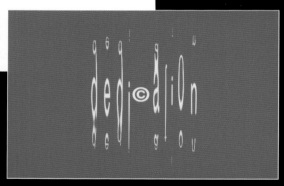

To challenge this reaction and to generate empathy for the issue, Digital Kitchen wanted to express the fundamental connection between the creative process and the final product by focusing on the artist. They used type and words such as 'practice', 'dedication', 'sacrifice' and 'respect' to symbolize the creative process of musical composition and performance. The sequence starts out rough, chaotic and undefined, like any artistic process, then inspiration, refinement and polish follow.

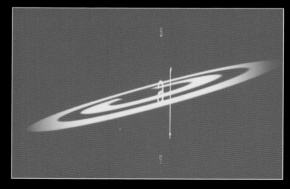

TITLE ARTISTS AGAINST PIRACY, © ACOUSTIC · FORMAT PUBLIC SERVICE ANNOUNCEMENT · ORIGIN USA · CLIENT ARTISTS AGAINST PIRACY · AGENCY DAILEY & ASSOCIATES · PRODUCTION, DESIGNER, DIRECTOR, MOTION GRAPHICS, EDITOR DIGITAL KITCHEN · MUSIC PRODUCTION DIGITAL KITCHEN WITH BRAD COLERICK · MUSIC PERFORMANCE BECK/GUITARIST LYLE WORKMAN

Overall, the message implies music's capacity to be a messenger for human emotion and personal vision. Digital Kitchen created two versions, 'electric' and 'unplugged' – shown here.

Audiovisual Essay

Students on the senior graphic design course taught by Nathalie Fallaha at the Lebanese American University in Beirut were asked to research thoroughly a topic of interest to them and to create a design solution that communicated the chosen message to an audience. It was up to each student to find the right medium, technique, typographic feel and imagery to best fulfil this brief.

Bruno Zalum's audiovisual essay *Purge* looks at trash, especially trash and the city, and specifically in Beirut. The essay is a trash can itself, into which he has thrown his ideas and beliefs about garbage, identity, reality, fiction, history, war, decomposition and cleanliness.

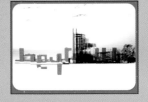

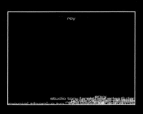

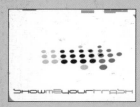

Working like an infernal machine that cannot stop growing, it takes Beirut to another dimension, face-to-face with her own reflection. A decomposed narrative style, mixed with a palette of different video-art, film-making and animation techniques creates a very

personal vision of detritus related to Beirut. But it is one that can be shared and interpreted by anyone for whom trash is more than just a banana skin.

 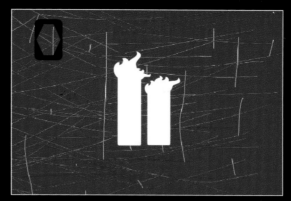

 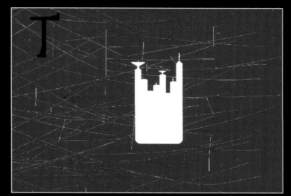

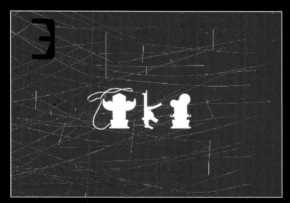 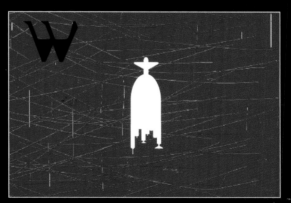

 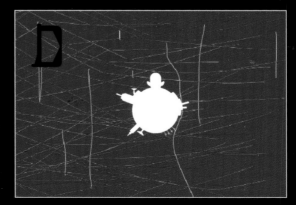

TITLE *PURGE* · **FORMAT** AUDIOVISUAL ESSAY · **ORIGIN** LEBANON ·
FACULTY ADVISOR NATHALIE FALLAHA · **DESIGNER, PRODUCTION**
BRUNO ZALUM

TITLE UNTITLED · **FORMAT** AUDIOVISUAL ESSAY · **ORIGIN** LEBANON ·
FACULTY ADVISOR NATHALIE FALLAHA · **DESIGNER, PRODUCTION**
LEA BADRO

Lea Badro's idea explored the notion of various objects of all shapes and forms superimposed onto one another to create new shapes and forms. By juxtaposing various objects, Badro created a typeface that alluded to recent wars. This representational, pictorial typeface creates sequences that illustrate various messages in a story-like form. Using this typeface, activists could spread their message on a global scale using a digital medium.

For this teaser campaign, FUEL's clients MTV did not want to reveal anything about what *Juice* was. Rather they wanted to publicize the name with an element of intrigue, in the style of motion-picture teasers, giving FUEL (see p. 26) the chance to do what they considered cool and would work for the MTV audience.

Type drives the creative sequences with an onslaught of on-screen adjectives provocatively declaring the spirit of *Juice*'s flowing, jumping, kinetic, fresh, raw, unstoppable power. Animated silhouettes suggest aspects of youth culture and lifestyle through dance and sports scenarios, without divulging the product's identity. The pace and visuals are quick and hard-hitting but also fun.

The ideas were expanded for two thirty-second spots, which used the style and attitude established in the teaser, but with a more surreal twist, simultaneously mixing two- and three-dimensional worlds.

It's
Halftime

to get 'em through the
2nd half.

And right **now**
one team has
already **lost.**

Nothing refuels
better.

Over **42** liters
of **SWEAT.**

Nothing replenishes
better.

At this rate
it'll take some
**serious
hydration**

is *it in you?*

INFORM
68

TITLE SWEAT · FORMAT PRODUCT PROMOTION · ORIGIN USA · CLIENT JAMESON MEDIA GROUP, LOS
RECTOR JUSTIN LEIBOW · DESIGNERS JUSTIN LEIBOW, KEVIN LAU, RICHARD ENG (LEBRON
JAMES SPOT) · ANIMATORS JUSTIN LEIBOW, KEVIN LAU, RICHARD ENG (LEBRON JAMES SPOT) · PRODUCER
JANET ARLOTTA · EDITOR CARSTEN BECKER · LIVE ACTION PRODUCER NANCY KISSOCK (LEBRON
SPOT) · DIRECTOR OF PHOTOGRAPHY PATRICK BARRON (LEBRON JAMES SPOT)

FORMAT PRODUCT PROMOTION · ORIGIN USA · CLIENT
ELEMENT 79 · CREATIVE DIRECTOR
JUSTIN LEIBOW · DESIGNERS REBEKAH BURCH, MIKE MACHIN · ANIMATOR MIKE MACHIN

The title of this commercial
is *Sweat* and that is exactly
what the type does. FUEL'S
artists modified, reworked,
textured and finally animated
a huge, slab-serif font to
make the letterforms sweat.
The typographic elements
embodied the brutal physical
strength needed to excel in
collegiate football.

Connecting the Dots

While this piece does not use a large quantity of type, typography plays an important role. Typographical elements enabled FUEL to simplify the message and communicate complex ideas succinctly. They used type in an iconographic way, so viewers did not have to actually read the words, instead their mind made immediate connections with larger themes as the words appeared. This allows the type to say more than there was time to express in the animation's voice over.

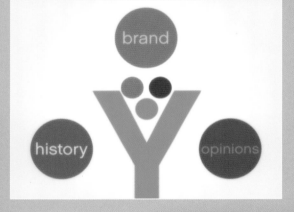

TITLE JWT · FORMAT PRODUCT PROMOTION · ORIGIN USA · CLIENT J. WALTER THOMPSON · CREATIVE DIRECTOR JUSTIN LEIBOW · DESIGNERS, ANIMATORS JUSTIN LEIBOW, JUAN MONASTERIO

TITLE TARGET VISA · FORMAT PRODUCT PROMOTION · ORIGIN USA · CLIENT PETERSON MILLA HOOKS · CREATIVE DIRECTOR, DESIGNER JUSTIN LEIBOW · ANIMATORS JUSTIN LEIBOW, JOHN ROCCO

GIVE CREDIT TO WHAT MATTERS MOST

TARGET.COM/VISA

The Bullseye Design is a registered trademark of Target Brands, Inc.

FUEL was asked to adapt the two-dimensional animations they had created for Target's earlier 'Sign of the Times' campaign into three-dimensional designs for Target's credit card and school benefit programme. The animated bull's-eye logo transforms into live-action images that pixilate into a three-dimensional galaxy of Target logos. During the animation it emerges that the logo is built up from the typography of thousands of words relating to learning and education, which connect the concepts of the sequence.

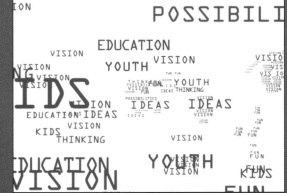

History Lessons

The time, motion and communication course taught by Professor Dan Boyarski at Carnegie Mellon's School of Design introduces students to time as a design element. Time allows for controlled sequencing and movement on screen, which is an effective format for communication design. These projects are thirty-second films that combine spoken words and visual elements to deliver information or to motivate the viewer to take action.

In response to all the boring school science films, Matt Tragesser wanted to create a piece that today's high-school students could relate to. Set to a lively James Brown soundtrack and the droll voice of a science teacher giving a lesson about Tungsten, the visuals complement the teaching. Words and images appear on screen in-sync with spoken words, to support the critical information. Informal tests have shown that audiences DO retain some of the information!

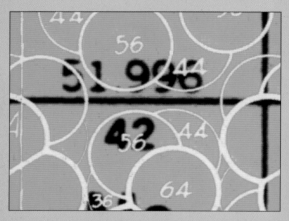

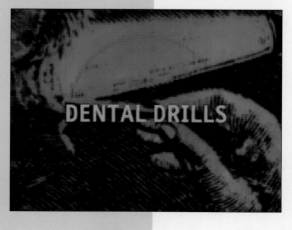

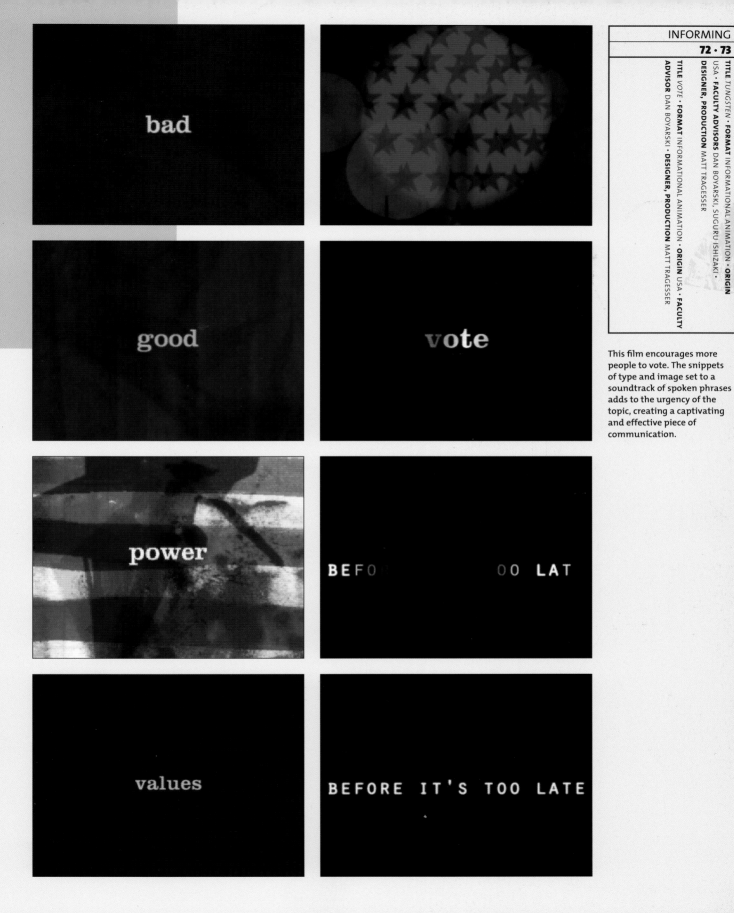

TITLE *TUNGSTEN* · **FORMAT** INFORMATIONAL ANIMATION · **ORIGIN** USA · **FACULTY ADVISORS** DAN BOYARSKI, SUGURU ISHIZAKI · **DESIGNER, PRODUCTION** MATT TRAGESSER

TITLE *VOTE* · **FORMAT** INFORMATIONAL ANIMATION · **ORIGIN** USA · **FACULTY ADVISOR** DAN BOYARSKI · **DESIGNER, PRODUCTION** MATT TRAGESSER

This film encourages more people to vote. The snippets of type and image set to a soundtrack of spoken phrases adds to the urgency of the topic, creating a captivating and effective piece of communication.

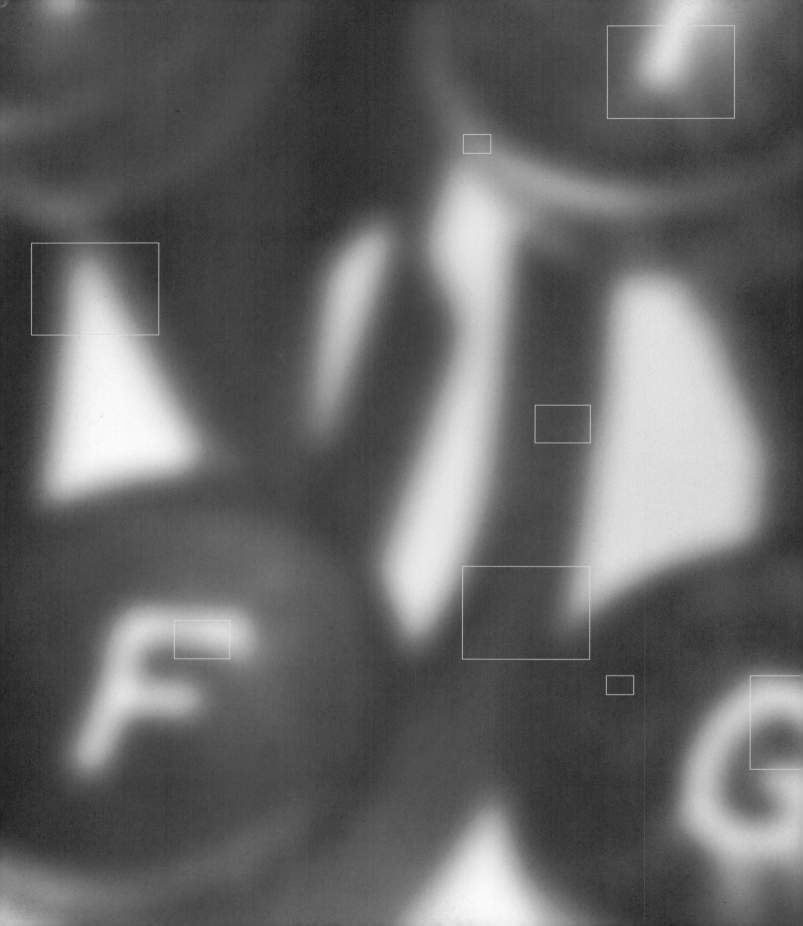

03　　Storytelling

Title sequences for films and television programmes are where time-based type and lettering is most visible as a means of storytelling, stitching together word, image and sound to create narratives and establish a context. This chapter, however, considers examples that go beyond passive narrative to encompass active storytelling, including kinetic poetry, emotional documentary and playful interaction. With interactive storytelling, the designer produces the conditions and framework for a story, but it is the user (or reader) who actually creates – and often becomes a part of – the narrative.

Bosnian-born Mirko Ilić began his career in Europe, illustrating and designing posters, record covers and comics, before moving to the USA in 1986 where he was commissioned as an illustrator for many leading magazines and newspapers. Following positions as art director of the international edition at *Time* magazine and art director of *The New York Times* Op-Ed pages, Ilić established Mirko Ilić Corp. in 1995, specializing in graphic design, three-dimensional computer graphics and motion-picture titles. In addition to his award-winning design and illustration work, Ilić has taught with Milton Glaser at Cooper Union and teaches master degree classes in illustration at the School of Visual Arts in New York.

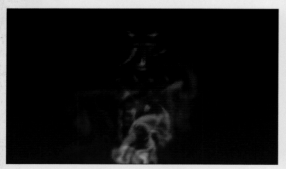

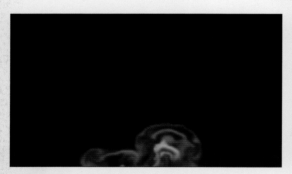

This title sequence for the short movie *Steamed Dumplings* was created using MAYA and without a budget. The movie's subject is the relationship between a Chinese person and an American. Ilić chose to represent the title by illustrating steam to create a visual metamorphosis of language. Beginning with Chinese characters, the studio manipulated them to produce a gradual visual transition into the English title.

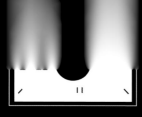

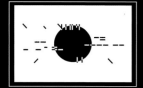

EAMED DUMPLINGS • **FORMAT** MAIN TITLE
CE • **ORIGIN** USA • **CLIENT** NEIL LEIFER • **ART**
ORS WALTER BERNARD, MIRKO ILIĆ • **ANIMATOR**
DENAPOLI • **STUDIOS** WBMG INC. AND MIRKO
P.

N STORIES • **FORMAT** MAIN TITLE SEQUENCE •
USA • **CLIENT** NEIL LEIFER • **ART DIRECTOR** MIRKO
SIGNERS MIRKO ILIĆ, HEATH HINEGARDNER •
MIRKO ILIĆ CORP.

This opening title for the independent movie *Zen Stories* was made using Adobe After Effects and with no budget. Ilić created a new typeface family that is able to fragment into horizontal, vertical and diagonal segments to mimic the perpetually changing, busy street environment of New York, where the story is set. The resulting sequence gives an intimate impression of the street atmosphere combined with a Zen aesthetic.

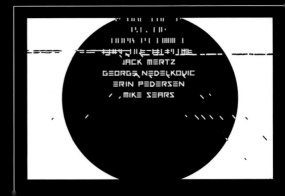

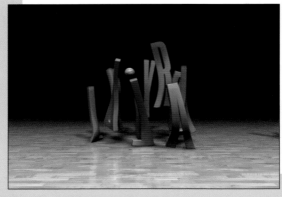

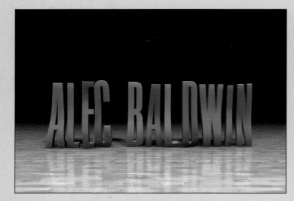

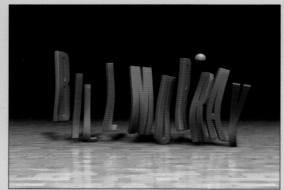

The limited budget allocated for the title design of the short movie *Scout's Honor* led Ilić to use Alias Wavefront. The theme of the movie, a basketball comedy, inspired Ilić to create basketball players from a typeface. Everything except for the ball and the court is designed from the face. The players' stance and gestures are emphasized by the animated movements of the letters across the screen (court). With the apostrophe representing the hoop, the players form into a line-up of text to create the movie's title.

Athletic Types

TITLE *SCOUT'S HONOR* · **FORMAT** MAIN TITLE SEQUENCE ·
ORIGIN USA · **CLIENT** NEIL LEIFER · **ART DIRECTORS**
WALTER BERNARD, MIRKO ILIĆ · **ANIMATOR** LAUREN
DENAPOLI · **STUDIOS** WBMG INC. AND MIRKO ILIĆ CORP.

TITLE *SMALLROOM DANCING* · **FORMAT** MAIN TITLE
SEQUENCE · **ORIGIN** USA · **CLIENT** NEIL LEIFER · **ART
DIRECTOR** MIRKO ILIĆ · **DESIGNERS** MIRKO ILIĆ, HEATH
HINEGARDNER · **STUDIOS** MIRKO ILIĆ CORP.

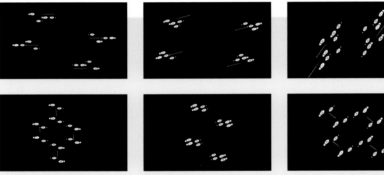

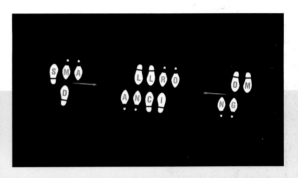

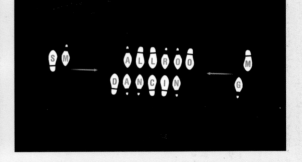

The opening sequence for
this short movie, *Smallroom
Dancing*, was created in
Adobe After Effects. The type
animation replicates the exact
dance steps of the foxtrot. As
the footsteps dance back and
forth across the screen, they
gradually reveal the movie's
title.

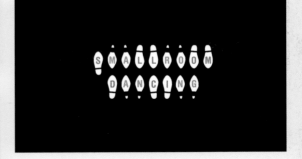

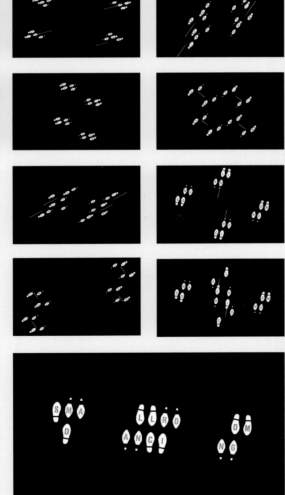

Personal to Universal

Students on the graphic design programme at the California College of the Arts, taught by assistant professor James Kenney, were given a project to produce a film that brought together a site of their choice and an assigned theory from an academic field, such as science, linguistics or media theory. Through the seemingly arbitrary intersection of site and theory, students were encouraged to construct new narratives that related to daily experiences and connected to universal themes.

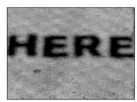

The site, a pedestrian bridge over a highway, is a transitional space under which traffic flows constantly. The film-maker questions the flexibility of his own identity, imagining that somewhere he is 'a farmer, an airplane pilot, a show girl; and somewhere, this road is a river.' All the typography in the film is composed as shadows.

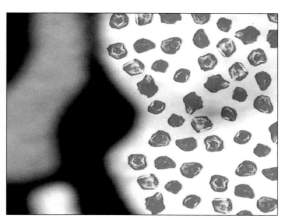

TITLE SOMEWHERE · **FORMAT** SHORT FILM · **ORIGIN** USA · **DIRECTOR, DESIGNER** ALEX DEARMOND

TITLE ALZHEIMER'S FILM · **FORMAT** SHORT FILM · **ORIGIN** USA · **DIRECTOR, DESIGNER** KRISTINA KARKANEN

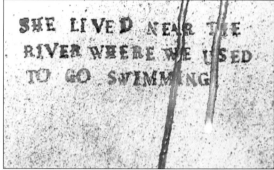

In this film, typography was hand-stamped onto a car window covered with condensation, revealing messages against sky and background scenery. As condensation drips through the words, their clarity is distorted, representing the ephemeral nature of memory. Scenes of hand-written post-it notes belonging to the film-maker's grandmother were also shown to juxtapose her gradual loss of memory through Alzheimer's disease with the film-maker's own fading image of her.

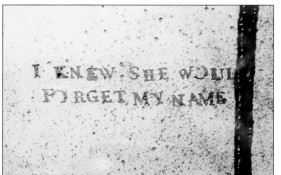

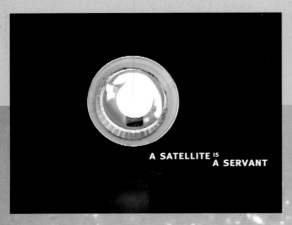

A SATELLITE **IS** A SERVANT

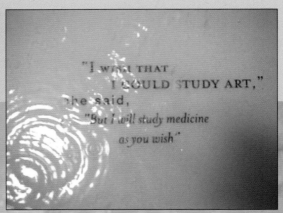

"I WISH THAT I COULD STUDY ART," she said, "But I will study medicine as you wish"

This film records a crucial turning point in the film-maker's life when she chose to follow her heart instead of her parents' plans for her. Using the definition of a satellite as 'a subservient follower', she compares her relationship with her parents to the relationship of the moon to the earth. As a satellite, the moon serves the earth, but the film-maker suggests that one day the moon may fly away. The typography in the film was produced both digitally and by filming type printed on various surfaces.

A MAN-MADE SATELLITE

THE MOON NATURAL OF THE EARTH

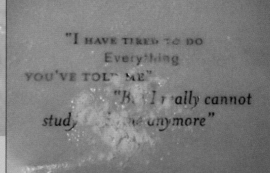

"I HAVE TRIED TO DO Everything YOU'VE TOLD ME" "But I really cannot study medicine anymore"

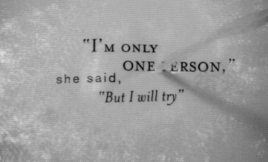

"I'M ONLY ONE PERSON," she said, "But I will try"

"But i need to leave" she said

ULTIMATELY THE EARTH'S GRAVITATIONAL PULL WILL CAUSE IT

THE MOON TRAVELS

INITIAL INERTIA

ONE DAY IT WILL EITHER FALL OR AWAY

TITLE SATELLITE · FORMAT SHORT FILM ·
ORIGIN USA · DIRECTOR, DESIGNER
HETTIE ZHANG

TITLE THE WILES OF OUR MINDS ·
FORMAT SHORT FILM · ORIGIN USA ·
DIRECTOR, DESIGNER JOYCE YU

The setting for this film is a
platform on an ocean beach
on which typography is being
physically washed away and
reprinted. Messages transform
with the continual cycles
of the tide, representing
the interchangeable nature
of memory.

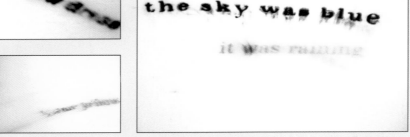

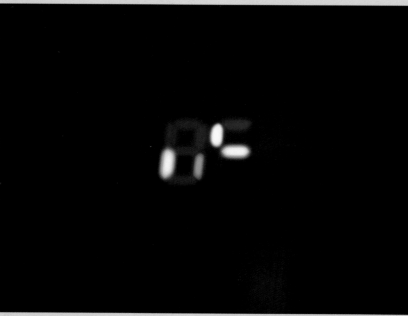

An unconventional title sequence for Fox's drama 24, starring Keifer Sutherland, conveys the key elements of the show: relentless action, suspense, intriguing mystery and the ever-present element of time. With just nine seconds to play with, Montgomery & Co. Creative (see p. 30) devised a minimalist LCD-clock logo.

They used Adobe Photoshop and Illustrator to create individual LCD segments, which eventually form into the number 24. Animated in Adobe After Effects, the segments were treated with glow and decay effects to mimic a real LCD display. Animating the individual segments produces a dramatic build-up, which culminates with the full revelation of the show's name.

The animated sequence was then filmed from a broadcast monitor and this was amalgamated with the original sequence to add an organic look. As a final touch, crystal glass elements were shot against a black background and incorporated into the title. This accentuated the climax of the sequence, while flash frames gave the impression of time elapsing and added to the viewer's suspense.

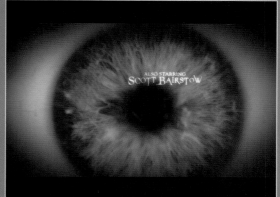

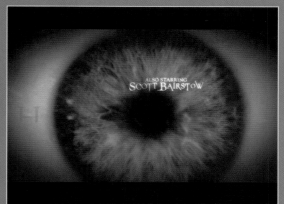

TITLE 24 · FORMAT MAIN TITLE SEQUENCE · ORIGIN USA · CLIENT FOX ·
EXECUTIVE CREATIVE DIRECTOR GEORGE MONTGOMERY · DESIGNER
MONTGOMERY & CO. CREATIVE

TITLE WOLF LAKE · FORMAT MAIN TITLE SEQUENCE · ORIGIN USA ·
CLIENT BIG TICKET TELEVISION AND CBS PRODUCTIONS · EXECUTIVE
CREATIVE DIRECTOR GEORGE MONTGOMERY · DESIGNER
MONTGOMERY & CO. CREATIVE

The CBS drama *Wolf Lake*, which stars Lou Diamond Phillips, is a series about a small, Pacific north-west town called Wolf Lake, where residents transform from humans into wolves.

The Emmy-nominated main title sequence avoided the traditional formula of character portraits, instead creating a journey that brought the viewers through the woods to the mystical and primal world of this fictional town and, finally, to the banks of the lake itself. Along the way, fragments of images introduce a sense of the characters, the setting and the dangers that await at Wolf Lake.

The typography reflects the idea of transformation; each title slowly evolves into a distressed and distorted style as elements of the type expand unnaturally. The vertical growth of each letter is reminiscent of a werewolf's fangs and claws. With its heartbeats and breathing, the background music adds to the haunting feel of the sequence.

Examining the Details

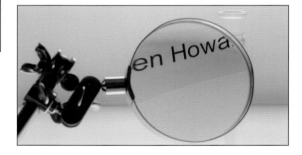

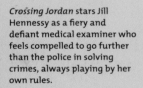

Crossing Jordan stars Jill Hennessy as a fiery and defiant medical examiner who feels compelled to go further than the police in solving crimes, always playing by her own rules.

Before designing the main title sequence, Montgomery & Co. Creative researched extensively the process of forensic examination, which included taking a tour of the Los Angeles County Coroner's office. Demonstrating the complex nature of a forensic examiner's work, the sequence takes viewers through a montage of stills of the tools of the trade, each one representing a character and his or her area of expertise.

Typography, a key element in the sequence, is integrated with these images. For example, the title is revealed through formaldehyde vapours, and, to reflect the sterile and scientific elements of examination, names were printed on acetate to create labels for the medical instruments. Finally, the closing credit includes a drop of blood exploding around the typography, suggesting the violent themes that are explored in the show.

TITLE *CROSSING JORDAN* · **FORMAT** MAIN TITLE SEQUENCE · **ORIGIN** USA ·
CLIENT NBC · **EXECUTIVE CREATIVE DIRECTOR** GEORGE MONTGOMERY ·
DESIGNER MONTGOMERY & CO. CREATIVE

TITLE *COYOTE UGLY* · **FORMAT** TRAILER · **ORIGIN** · USA · **CLIENT** DISNEY ·
EXECUTIVE CREATIVE DIRECTOR GEORGE MONTGOMERY · **DESIGNER**
MONTGOMERY & CO. CREATIVE

Bar-room Banter

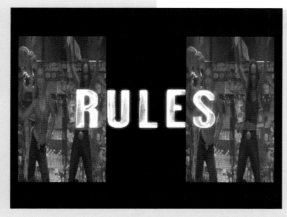

Provocative words and
phrases overlay quick-cut
action scenes from inside
the infamous women-
operated New York drinking
establishment, *Coyote Ugly*,
in these advertisements for
the film of the same name.
Montgomery & Co. created
hand-painted textures to fill in
the typography and add to the
country-and-western infused,
big-city setting.

Capturing the Classics

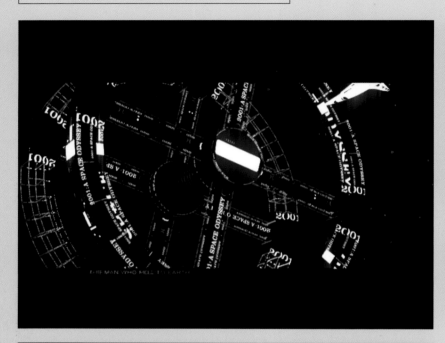

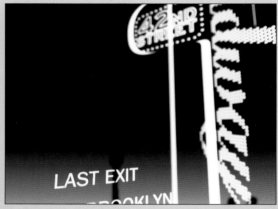

The Grand Classics is a film festival where actors and directors show their favourite movies. To introduce the shows, Trollbäck & Company designed title sequences that recreate iconic movie scenes using typography. The scenes were rebuilt as computer graphics so that type could be mapped onto the images. By using text and famous imagery, the sequences convey the festival's central theme: 'the power of film to inspire'.

The title sequence for director Gary Winick's acclaimed independent feature shows a shoal of letters swimming along like tadpoles. The letters form the opening credits against the backdrop of outdoor landscapes, as if viewed from a speeding car.

'Because of the changes being made to the film, there was a lot of back and forth,' said Trollbäck's creative director, Nathalie de la Gorce. 'We were very enthusiastic about the film and the director, so we worked hard and fast – the best way – to design titles.'

TITLE THE GRAND CLASSICS · **FORMAT** MAIN TITLE SEQUENCE · **ORIGIN** USA · **CLIENT** AMERICAN FILM INSTITUTE · **CREATIVE DIRECTORS** JAKOB TROLLBÄCK, NATHALIE DE LA GORCE · **EDITOR** NICOLE AMATO

TITLE *TADPOLE* · **FORMAT** MAIN TITLE SEQUENCE · **ORIGIN** USA · **CLIENT** INDIGENT PRODUCTIONS · **CREATIVE DIRECTORS** NATHALIE DE LA GORCE, LAURENT FAUCHERE · **3D ANIMATOR** CHRIS HAAK · **ANIMATOR** JASMIN JODRY · **FEATURE FILM DIRECTOR** GARY WINICK

Tadpole, which stars Sigourney Weaver, John Ritter, Bebe Neuwirth and Robert Iler, tells the story of a brilliant, sophisticated fifteen-year-old boy who falls in love with his step-mother.

Blind Type

In this Emmy Award–winning title sequence, Uma Thurman's character is being examined for hysterical blindness. Wanting the viewer to experience the examination from the character's viewpoint, Trollbäck & Company showed blinding light and darkness intertwined. To achieve this, they pulled in and out of focus and used flashlights shot on digital video to provide organic light-source effects. An eye chart was used for the main title card.

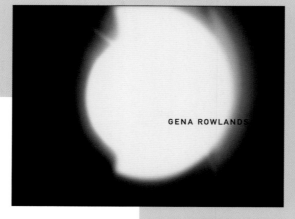

Visual Poetry

In the opening title sequence for *Vanity Fair*, Trollbäck & Company incorporated vivid icons for the film's central motifs: money and greed, vanity, beauty and Orientalism. Shot in the purest visual language, the dream-like sequence shows crisp, hyper-realistic images.

TITLE *HYSTERICAL BLINDNESS* · FORMAT MAIN TITLE SEQUENCE · ORIGIN USA · CLIENT HBO FILMS · DIRECTOR JAKOB TROLLBÄCK · CREATIVE DIRECTORS ANTOINE TINGUELY, LAURENT FAUCHERE · EDITOR NICOLE AMATO · TECHNICAL DIRECTOR CHRIS HAAK

TITLE *VANITY FAIR* · FORMAT MAIN TITLE SEQUENCE · ORIGIN USA · CLIENT MIRABAI FILMS · TROLLBÄCK & COMPANY: DIRECTORS JAKOB TROLLBÄCK, JOE WRIGHT · CREATIVE DIRECTOR, ART DIRECTOR JOE WRIGHT · DESIGNER TESIA JURKIEWICZ · TECHNICAL DIRECTOR CHRIS HAAK · EDITOR CASS VANINI · ASSISTANT PRODUCER ELIZABETH KIEHNER · EXECUTIVE PRODUCER JULIE SHEVACH · MIRABAI FILMS: DIRECTOR MIRA NAIR · EDITOR ALLYSON C. JOHNSON · ASSISTANT EDITOR DAVID SMITH · POST SUPERVISOR JENNIFER FREED · DIRECTOR OF PHOTOGRAPHY DECLAN QUINN · ADDITIONAL PHOTOGRAPHY STUART DRYBURGH · COMPOSER MYCHAEL DANNA · VENDOR COMPANIES NEGATIVE SCAN, COLOUR CORRECT & FILM OUT: E FILM

Lyrical Movement

Headed by James Kenney, InterStitch Films produces animations, title designs and experimental short films. Kenney is also assistant professor at California College of the Arts, and his work has featured in publications, such as *ID* magazine, and festivals, including ResFest Digital Film Festival. He has been honoured by The Type Directors Club of America and The American Institute of Graphic Artists.

The title sequence begins in the air with the 'baby lift' from Vietnam. Then letterforms lyrically blow into place and out again, incorporating part of the title translated into Nom characters, the traditional written language of Vietnam. The sequence ends with a shot of a warm beach in Vietnam where Heidi's mother is searching for her.

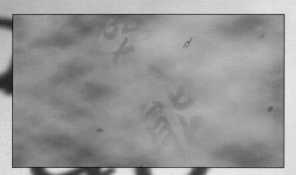

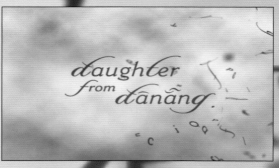

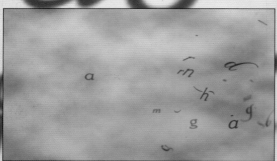

InterStitch created a main title sequence for the documentary *Daughter from Danang*, which won the Grand Jury Prize at the Sundance Film Festival in 2002 and was nominated for an Academy Award in 2003. The film follows the experience Heidi, who was adopted by a family in the USA at the end of the Vietnam War and later goes back to Vietnam to find her family.

TITLE *DAUGHTER FROM DANANG* · **FORMAT** MAIN TITLE SEQUENCE · **ORIGIN** USA · **CLIENT** INTERFAZE PRODUCTIONS · **ART DIRECTOR, DESIGNER** JAMES KENNEY

TITLE *AGING IN AMERICA* · **FORMAT** MAIN TITLE SEQUENCE · **ORIGIN** USA · **CLIENT** TALKING EYES MEDIA · **ART DIRECTOR, DESIGNER** JAMES KENNEY

Ageless Elegance

A seven-year project, the documentary *Aging in America* chronicled the varied perspectives of the elderly population across the country. Thousands of photographs were taken for the film, which the title sequence used, cropping them selectively to magnify the marks deposited by time. Not wanting to promote a depressing representation of aging, the director and designer employed vibrant colours, contemporary typography and lively animation.

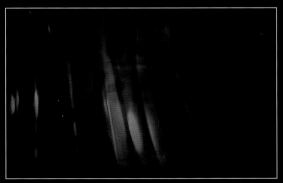

Formal Dissection

InterStitch created this sequence for the San Francisco chapter of the American Institute of Graphic Arts (AIGA) to promote a lecture series and to announce upcoming speakers. The piece uses a combination of analogue and digital design. Adobe After Effects was used to add animated graphics and three-dimensional layered elements to a digital video. The lecture series discussed the topics of truth and beauty, themes depicted in the sequence by its dissection and reconstruction of forms.

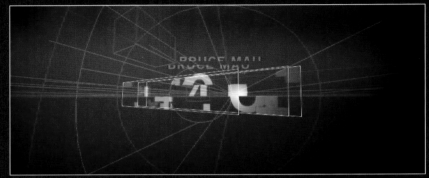

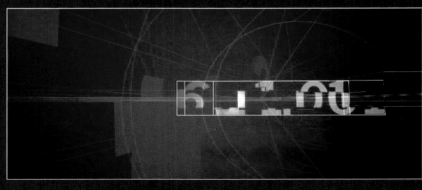

Counterformal Synthesis

BUSINESS

BRIO.
THE BUSINESS PERFORMANCE
SOFTWARE COMPANY.

STORYTELLING

94 · 95

TITLE AIGA LECTURE SERIES · **FORMAT** PROMOTION · **ORIGIN** USA ·
CLIENT AIGA, SAN FRANCISCO CHAPTER · **ART DIRECTOR, DESIGNER**
JAMES KENNEY

TITLE *BRIO* · **FORMAT** PROMOTION · **ORIGIN** *USA* · **CLIENT** *BRIO* · **ART
DIRECTOR, DESIGNER** JAMES KENNEY

To promote the character
and energy of a software
development company,
InterStitch created this
promotional sequence for
them to use internally and
externally. Using only two
colours and one typeface, the
video plays with the level of
innovation and surprise that
can be found within such a
simple system. In this way, the
sequence's form represents
the efficiency of the client's
products.

Visualizing Conversation

British designer and animator Garry Waller currently works in New York. Enjoying the freedom to work outside the commercial sphere, he experiments with type and audio recordings, rarely leaving home without a mini-disc recorder in his bag.

London is a short animation that uses animated type to a soundtrack of conversations of survivors of the blitz in London during the Second World War. Throughout, type is in constant motion: fading, jumping, blurring, scrolling or exploding in-sync with the dialogues to enhance the expressive and often lively accounts.

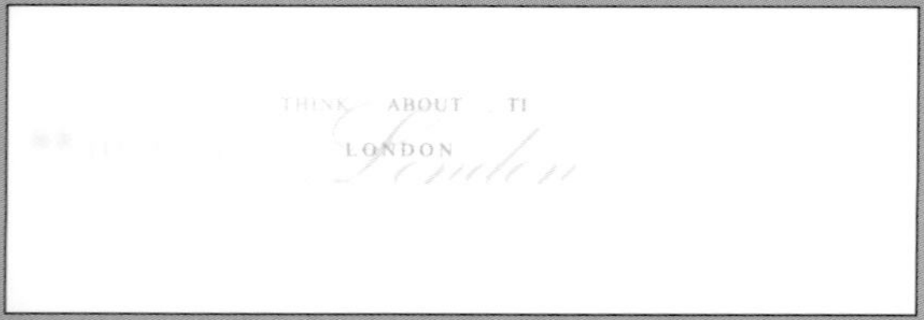

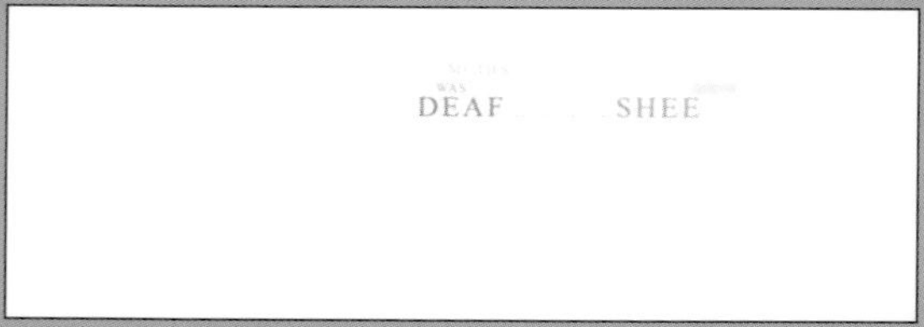

TRA FALG SQUARE

ON
NEW

" BOMBING

" BOMBING

THINK ABOUT TI
LONDON

RAP NELL W'ZZ
FALLING

LONDON   LONDON

nall   ev ree hhware

BOMBING

DEAF   SHEE

TRA FALG SQUARE THE HOLE'VE

oughh!
REEL IYZE
REALLY

SHHHH
REALLY

v • FORMAT DIGITAL
ORIGIN UK • DIRECTOR,
DESIGNER, PRODUCTION GARRY WALLER

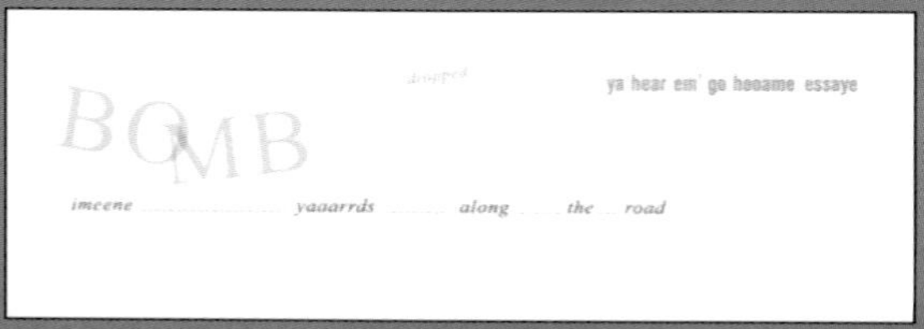

SHHHH

PSHHH PSHEH

PSHHH SHEWZZ

REALLY

aughter

PSHHH SHHHH SHHHH

FRIEND WEL'SS
she was
GROVELLING

she wanted

SHEWZZ IN SUCH A STATE

right IN THEE air

vOoO
my muh wenaayh aughter

INTO
THE
SHELTER

along one passage
—TO THE SHELTER
and shee flungher arms

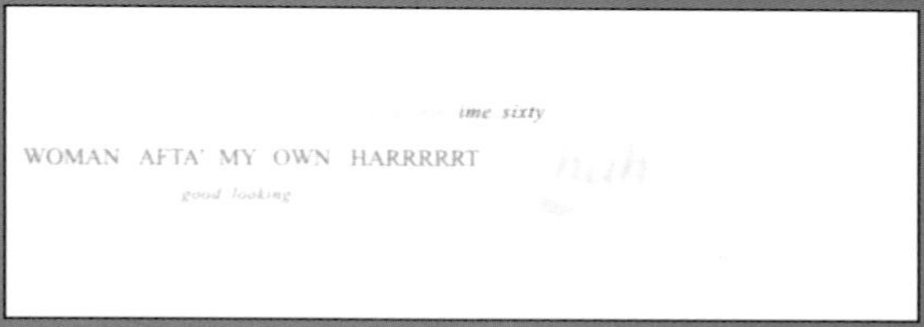

THAT THIS WOZZEN THE norm

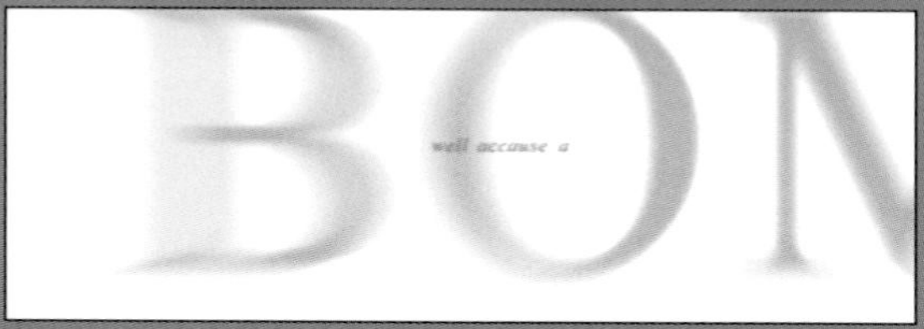

me sixty
WOMAN AFTA' MY OWN HARRRRRT
good looking

BOMB

well because a

THE
O L E

BIGGEST stranger in London

a dropped
BOMB
imeene

THE
WHOLE'VE

in London

dropped ya hear em go haoame essaye
BOMB
imeene yaaarrds along the road

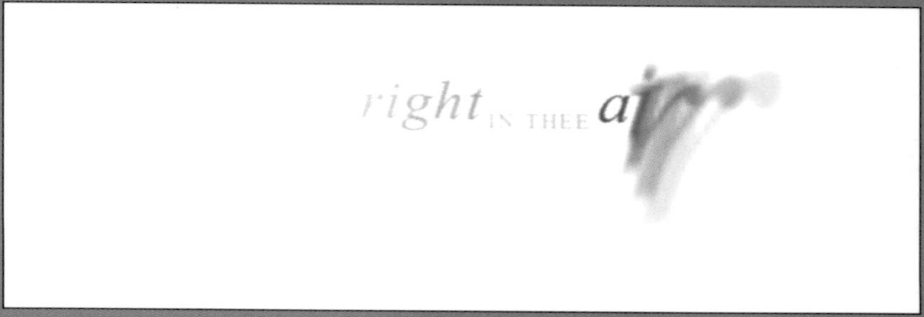

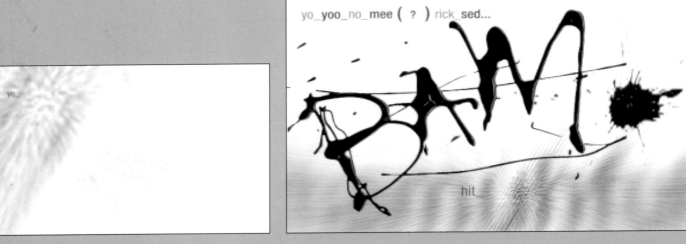

After witnessing a street fight break out in the East Village, New York, Waller recorded the aftermath, which offered a compelling narrative. The resulting piece, *You Know Mee*, is a short type animation that depicts one man's violent exaggerations as he recounts his victory to his friends.

TITLE *YOU KNOW MEE* · FORMAT DIGITAL ANIMATION · ORIGIN UK · DIRECTOR, DESIGNER, PRODUCTION GARRY WALLER

Taming the Type

Born in Rio de Janeiro, Roberto de Vicq de Cumptich received a BA in graphic design in Brazil and then won a painting scholarship to the Pratt Institute in New York, where he completed his MFA in 1984. He is senior creative director and vice president at HarperCollins, where he oversees the design of more than 800 books a year, personally designing between 100 and 150 of them. In 2003, his designs for *Lucky Girls* and *Krakatoa* were winners in the AIGA 50 Books/50 Covers juried exhibition.

Matteo Bologna, from Milan, founded Mucca Design in New York in 1999. Mucca (pronounced moo-kah) is Italian for cow, although the name probably is not what attracted the fashionable restaurant clientele that the studio is popular with. Bologna is also the transatlantic art director for Italian publisher Rizzoli Libri and several imprints of HarperCollins. Mucca designs more than 500 books and covers per year.

Bison

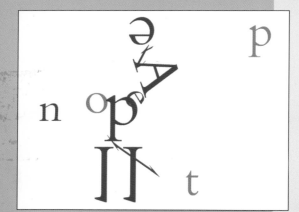

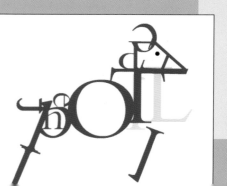

Antelope

Crab

Bembo's Zoo is an abecedary featuring a menagerie of animals, each created from all the letters in its name and using the Bembo font. Its success inspired de Vicq to collaborate with Bologna on an interactive website to bring the book to life, allowing the visitor to watch the animals form from letters.

TITLE *BEMBO'S ZOO* · **FORMAT** WEBSITE AND
PRINTED BOOK · **ORIGIN** USA · **PUBLISHER**
HENRY HOLT AND COMPANY · **CREATIVE**
DESIGNERS, PRODUCTION ROBERTO DE VICQ
DE CUMPTICH, MUCCA DESIGN,
FEDERICO CHIELI

Yak

Zebra

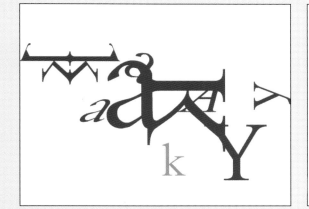

Type Faces

STOP A WRY LAD	TRY A SLOW PAD	A WORDY SPLAT
DRAW A SLY TOP	AT SWORDPLAY	STOP A DRY LAW
WARY POST LAD	A PATSY WORLD	A LOW DRY SPAT
SPRAWL TODAY	PLATO WAS DRY	WORST PLAY AD
OLD SATYR PAW	OSWALD PARTY	PART OLD WAYS

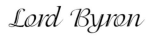

Lord Byron

Twenty-five OpenType fonts from the Adobe Type Library were used to create portraits for this website and accompanying printed book entitled *Words at Play*. In Flaubert's portrait, Nuptial Script becomes a tongue-in-cheek tribute to the writer who vivisected marriage with a sharp nib; Poetica's flowing lines capture Herman Melvill's weathered features; and Kafka's portrait uses Quake to create an image that reverberates with raw angst. This trio of fonts exemplifies the evocative power of the OpenType fonts, testimony to the re-birth of the highest typographic ideals that are evident in *Words at Play*.

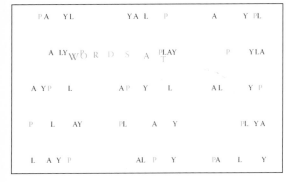

What's in store? Punderful quotes about provocative features.
[Hintriguing!]

WORDS AT PLAY

"But words are things,
and a small drop of ink,
Falling like dew
upon a thought, produces
That which makes thousands,
perhaps millions, think."

TITLE WORDS AT PLAY · **FORMAT** WEBSITE AND PRINTED BOOK · **ORIGIN** USA · **SPONSORS** ADOBE SYSTEMS, INC., YUPO CORPORATION — AMERICA, ANDREWS CONNECTICUT · **CREATIVE DESIGNERS, PRODUCTION** ROBERTO DE VICQ DE CUMPTICH, MATTEO BOLOGNA

"UTTER ING A
IS
THE LIKE A
KEY
BOARD
IMAG TION"
INA

A WORD NOTE ON
O F THE

Ludwig Wittgenstein 1889–1951

Gustave Flaubert

Herman Melville

Franz Kafka

DOROTHY PARKER

"I CAN'T WRITE FIVE WORDS BUT THAT I CHANGE SEVEN."

Dorothy Parker 1893–1967

EDGAR ALLAN POE

Edgar Allan Poe 1809–1849

"POETRY IS THE RHYTHMICAL CREATION OF BEAUTY IN WORDS."

AL CAPONE

"You can get much farther with a kind word and a gun than you can with a kind word alone."

Al Capone 1899–1947

JEAN-PAUL SARTRE

"Words are loaded pistols."

Jean-Paul Sartre 1905–1980

OLIVER WENDELL HOLMES

"Life and language are alike sacred. Homicide and verbicide—that is, violent treatment of a word with fatal results to its legitimate meaning, which is its life—are alike forbidden."

Oliver Wendell Holmes 1809–1894

JOSEPH CONRAD

"A word carries far; very far; deals destruction through time as the bullets go flying through space."

Joseph Conrad 1857–1924

Gestural Reality

For this music video, Foreign Office (see p. 62) was asked to create colourful, animated spray-can graffiti backgrounds on a tight budget and with little time. They used the artist M.I.A.'s original artwork and also created new graphics using spray paint.

Graphics were scanned in, coloured and animated using Adobe After Effects. The studio worked closely with director Ruben Fleischer and M.I.A., taking great care to retain the handmade raw 'ghetto' style of the song in the video. Themes of tropical birds, tigers, textile patterns and guerilla-style warfare were explored, many inspired by the artist's native Sri Lanka.

TITLE GALANG · FORMAT MUSIC VIDEO · ORIGIN UK · ARTIST M.I.A. · CLIENT XL
RECORDINGS UK · DIRECTOR RUBEN FLEISCHER · PRODUCER DAVIDE STEWART ·
PRODUCTION COMPANY PARTIZAN · ANIMATOR FOREIGN OFFICE, VTR

TITLE STORY OF BLUE GURU · FORMAT WEBSITE · ORIGIN UK · CLIENT BLUE
GURU · DIRECTOR, ANIMATOR, SOUND DESIGN FOREIGN OFFICE

As part of its marketing
campaign, up-and-coming
fashion label Blue Guru wrote
a short story about the genesis
of their jeans. Looking to
ancient India for inspiration,
Foreign Office created a
flowing, abstract film and a
voiceover track to illustrate
the story. Some graphics were
borrowed from the brand's
T-shirt motifs, but most were
made from scratch, giving the
piece a branded, but absurd,
surreal feel. Bizarre humour
was very important for the
studio, and a mysterious, dark
tone was chosen for the type,
graphics and animation.

Story Lines

These projects were created on the time, motion and communication course at Carnegie Mellon University's School of Design (see p. 72). The objective was to use animated type to express visually a passage from a literary work, a poem, a song lyric or a spoken monologue, with the emphasis on evoking the voice of the author.

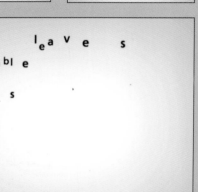

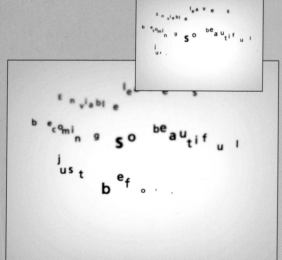

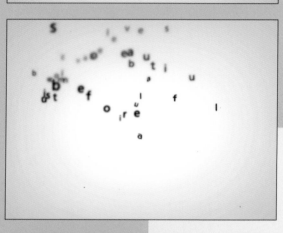

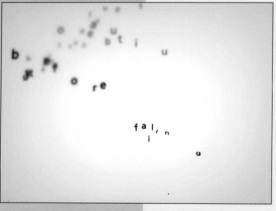

This is a visual representation of a haiku about falling leaves. The letters (leaves) are in constant motion and at key moments they position themselves to spell a word. The sequence ends with the final word falling and blowing away.

TITLE *HAIKU* · **FORMAT** NARRATIVE ANIMATION · **ORIGIN** USA · **FACULTY ADVISOR** DAN BOYARSKI · **DESIGNER, PRODUCTION** HEEBOK LEE

TITLE *THE LITTLE BOY AND THE OLD MAN* · **FORMAT** NARRATIVE ANIMATION · **ORIGIN** USA · **FACULTY ADVISOR** DAN BOYARSKI · **DESIGNER, PRODUCTION** JACK MOFFETT

The **Little** **Boy** **And** **The** **Old** **Man**

By Shel Silverstein

"I **wet**my pants."

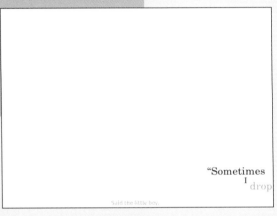

"Sometimes I drop

Said the little boy.

"But **worst** of **all**," "it seems,"

Said the boy.

Said the little old man,

" **I** do

"Grown-don't ups pay **attention** to " me.

" **I** do that " **too.**

"I **know** what " you mean,

A heartfelt poem by Shel Silverstein, this dialogue between a little boy and an old man is given visual voice using kinetic typography. The behaviour of individual words entering and exiting the screen reflects the pattern of spoken words so that you begin to 'hear' the individual voices. Timing, choice of typeface and position on the screen are critical to conveying a specific voice.

FOOSBALL soccer soccer then two

FOOSBALL and I ~~~~ guys

is soccer thought around look

a shishkabobs you cannot like

combination FOOSBALL had do me

of screwed up to backflip me

soccer my kick backflip men me me me me me me me

soccer preception ball several me me me me me me me me me me me me me me
                              several me

and of simultaneously me me me me me me me me me me me me me me me me

TITLE *FOOSBALL* · **FORMAT** NARRATIVE
ANIMATION · **ORIGIN** USA · **FACULTY**
ADVISOR DAN BOYARSKI · **DESIGNER,**
PRODUCTION TIM FIFE

TITLE *ON THE ROAD* **FORMAT** NARRATIVE
ANIMATION · **ORIGIN** USA · **FACULTY**
ADVISOR DAN BOYARSKI · **DESIGNER,**
PRODUCTION JIM KENNEY

Set to a lively jazz riff by Charles Mingus, the monologue (opposite) is about the differences between soccer and foosball. Connecting the movement of the words with their meanings adds to the humour of the piece.

In an attempt to capture the frenetic writing style of Jack Kerouac's *On the Road*, the words fly on and off screen, responding to a jazz piece by Miles Davis and John Coltrane. Readability is sometimes sacrificed in favour of setting the mood of the 1950s and the overall feel of the text.

This two-minute animated title sequence for the motion picture, *Secondhand Lions*, appears at the end of the film. Written and directed by Tim McCanlies and starring Haley Joel Osment, Michael Caine and Robert Duvall, the movie is a about the bonds that develop when a shy and cynical boy visits his two eccentric great uncles one summer in Texas.

Digital Kitchen (see p. 36) created an opening title sequence that visually captures the whimsy of the movie *A Guy Thing*, in which a young groom-to-be must choose between the 'right thing' and the 'real thing' when he falls for his fiancée's free-spirited cousin. The sequence opens with a band playing a late-night set, followed by a short exchange between the main character and his friend, who is offering support as his wedding day approaches.

Music begins and the scene changes to Seattle's cityscape at dawn as the credits appear. A series of coloured mosaics forms patterns over the footage, reminiscent of Saul Bass's titles for *The Man with the Golden Arm* and *Anatomy of a Murder*. The sequence finishes with a shot of the main character asleep, setting the scene for the film.

TITLE A *GUY THING* · **FORMAT** IDENTITY SEQUENCE · **ORIGIN** USA · **CLIENT** METRO-GOLDWYN-MAYER PICTURES · **PRODUCTION, DESIGNER, DIRECTOR, MOTION GRAPHICS, EDITOR** DIGITAL KITCHEN

TITLE *SECONDHAND LIONS* · **FORMAT** IDENTITY SEQUENCE · **ORIGIN** USA · **CLIENT** NEW LINE CINEMA · **PRODUCTION, DESIGNER, DIRECTOR, MOTION GRAPHICS, EDITOR** DIGITAL KITCHEN

Using original artwork from Pulitzer Prize–winning cartoonist Berkeley Breathed (*Bloom County*) as a template, Digital Kitchen imported a variety of images – in comic-strip ink and paint – and assembled them into magical three-dimensional titles.

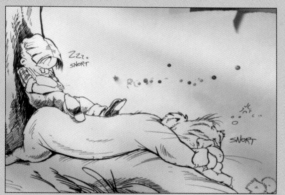

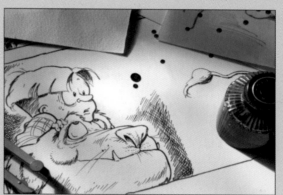

The whimsical, sophisticated sequence is unique in that the credits emerge from the actual 'work space' of Osment's character, Walter, as a grown up. The animated piece is another scene in the movie, telling the story of the main character's profession. The result is an original and dynamic title sequence that reflects the humour and tone of the film.

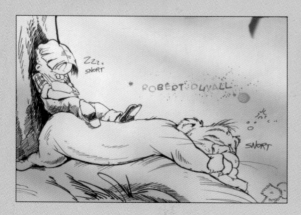

Strictly Business

Hitoshi Takekiyo's career involves both the teaching and the practice of design. After several years as a tutor at Kobe Art University, Japan, he established Koo-Ki Motion Graphics (see p. 48) in 1997, which specializes in motion graphics for television and film. KeeJung Kwon joined Koo-Ki in 2004, where he works as a motion graphic designer.

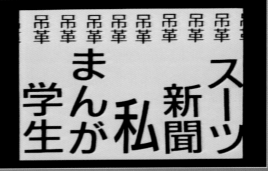

Banana is a short film that uses only letters (code) to represent a typical day for a Japanese businessman. It is not intended to be a futurist expression, but an interpretation of a human's visual ability to capture an environment as code.

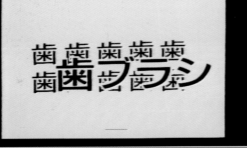

TITLE BANANA · **FORMAT** DIGITAL
ANIMATION · **ORIGIN** JAPAN · **DESIGNER,**
PRODUCTION HITOSHI TAKEKIYO

TITLE OOZE, JAM, GUSH · **FORMAT** DIGITAL
ANIMATION · **ORIGIN** JAPAN · **DESIGNER,**
PRODUCTION KEEJUNG KWON

Erotica

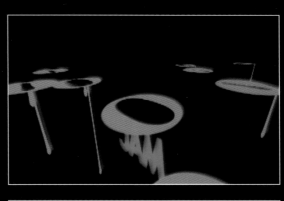

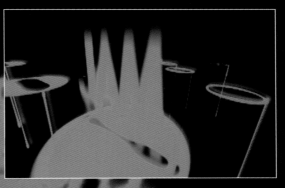

This one-minute-twenty-
second animation visualizes
the meaning of words through
typography. Through graphic
manipulation and movement,
three words – *ooze, jam,
gush* – collectively evoke an
erotic mood.

Documenting Megalomania

John Underkoffler is a science and technology advisor for film productions, which have included *Minority Report*, *The Hulk*, the mini-series *Taken*, and the live-action adaptation *Aeon Flux*. He specializes in developing plausible technologies for futuristic or fictional environments, basing them on contemporary processes and techniques, so they are grounded in the present and believable.

Before working in Los Angeles, Underkoffler was a researcher at MIT's Media Lab for fifteen years, where he earned three degrees. He worked with the spatial imaging group and was responsible for innovations in optical and electronic holography, and with the tangible media group, which developed systems that aimed to create architectural spaces where every surface could display and collect visual information.

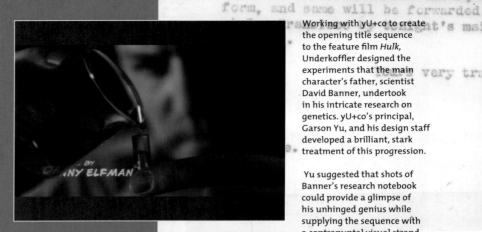

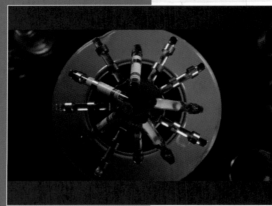

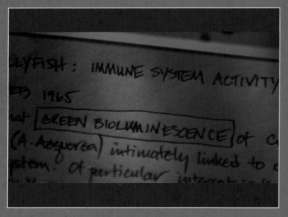

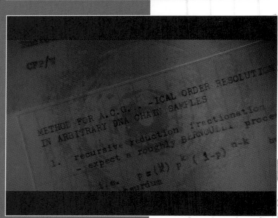

Working with yU+co to create the opening title sequence to the feature film *Hulk*, Underkoffler designed the experiments that the main character's father, scientist David Banner, undertook in his intricate research on genetics. yU+co's principal, Garson Yu, and his design staff developed a brilliant, stark treatment of this progression.

Yu suggested that shots of Banner's research notebook could provide a glimpse of his unhinged genius while supplying the sequence with a contrapuntal visual strand. So a research notebook was required. Underkoffler composed a chronological series of entries, intended to communicate the essence of Banner's experiments as well as the twisted-philosophy-fuelled megalomania driving the work. He and yU+co's designers laid out the pages with appropriate imagery, diagrams and other visual elements. Underkoffler then penned the pages' content – most of it in advance but some of it 'live' on camera – in a disconnected longhand he had developed to evoke comic-book lettering while still appearing plausibly 'personal'.

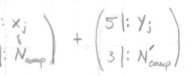

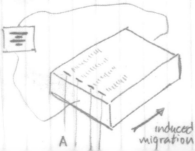

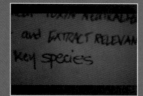

TITLE HULK · **FORMAT** MAIN TITLE SEQUENCE · **ORIGIN** USA · **CLIENT** ANG LEE / UNIVERSAL PICTURES · **PRODUCTION COMPANY** YU+CO · **PRODUCER** JENNIFER FONG · **EXPERIMENT & EQUIPMENT DESIGNER, BANNER'S NOTEBOOK TEXT, DESIGNER, HANDWRITING** JOHN UNDERKOFFLER · **CREATIVE DIRECTOR** GARSON YU · **INFERNO ARTIST** CONNY FAUSER · **2D TYPE ANIMATOR** ETSUKO UJI · **2D DESIGNER** SYNDERELA PENG · **EDITOR** EMMY LEUNG, TONY FULGHAM · **CINEMATOGRAPHERS** FRED ELMES, TOMMY LOHMANN

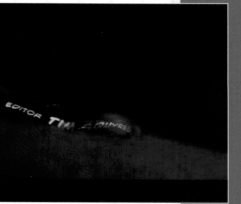

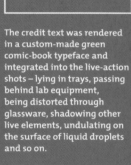

The credit text was rendered in a custom-made green comic-book typeface and integrated into the live-action shots – lying in trays, passing behind lab equipment, being distorted through glassware, shadowing other live elements, undulating on the surface of liquid droplets and so on.

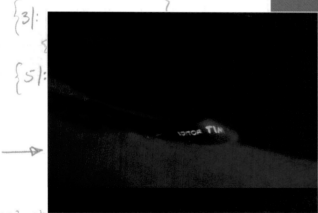

The title sequence is a staccato filmstrip of stylized mad-scientist imagery showing David Banner working his way up the evolutionary chain, 'Frankensteining' together genetic bits and pieces into an inadvisable broth he would self-administer and then inadvertently pass along to his son Bruce.

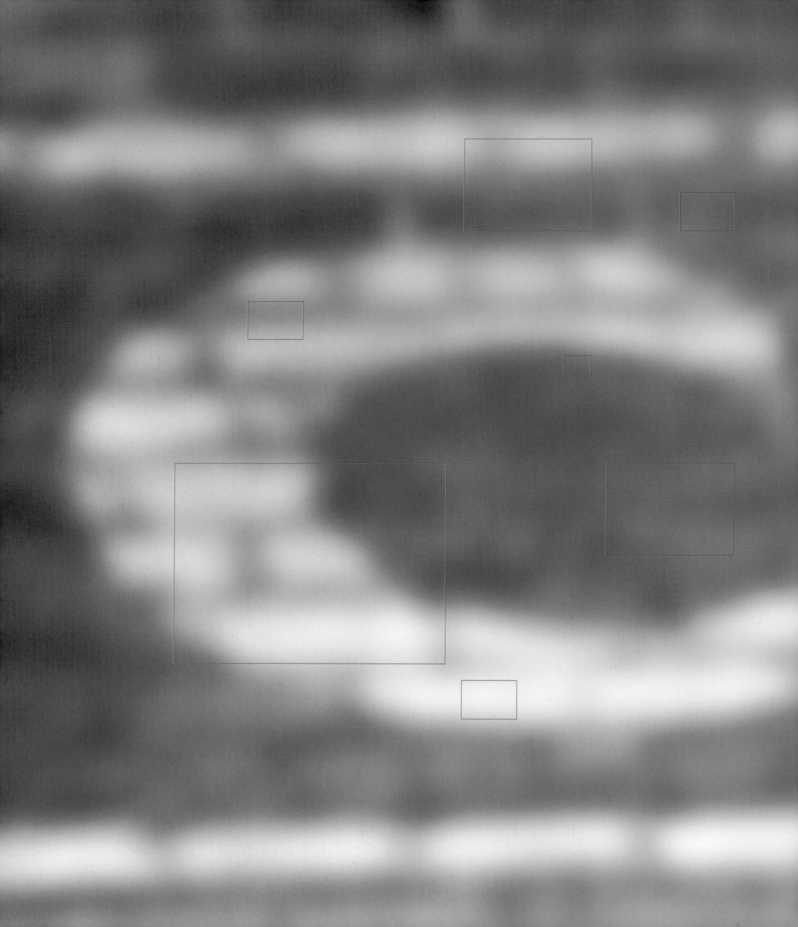

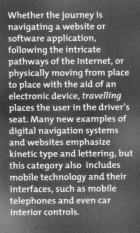

Whether the journey is navigating a website or software application, following the intricate pathways of the Internet, or physically moving from place to place with the aid of an electronic device, *travelling* places the user in the driver's seat. Many new examples of digital navigation systems and websites emphasize kinetic type and lettering, but this category also includes mobile technology and their interfaces, such as mobile telephones and even car interior controls.

Icons in Motion

Japan-based Ten_Do_Ten works exclusively in the infant field of design for mobile-phone screens. The relatively low resolution and small dimension of the screen may seem an uninteresting medium in which to produce creative motion design, but the highly interactive nature of phone technology – a synthesis of computer programming with visual design – creates limitless potential when the end user participates in the design outcome.

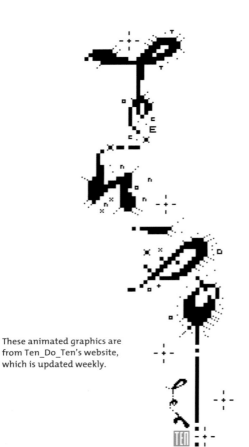

These animated graphics are from Ten_Do_Ten's website, which is updated weekly.

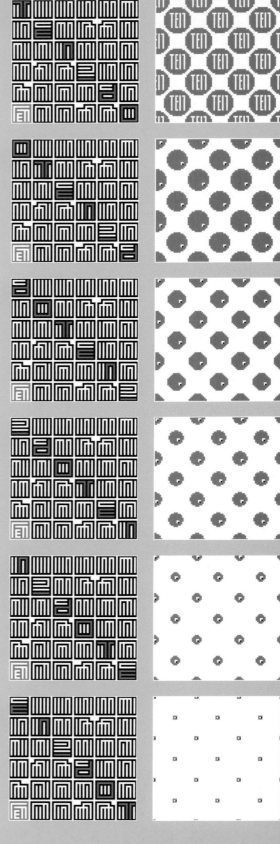

my name is ten.
ten means pixel in japanese.
ten is a meaning called a pixel
in Japanese.
ten can be drawn on anyone.
ten may be unable to be
drawn on anybody.
ten may be understood also by
the alien.
ten may be understood only in
human beings.
ten may be understood only
by Japanese people.
ten may be understood only
by you!

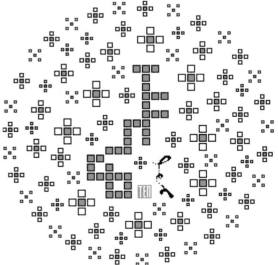

These screen animations were
designed for MTV Mobile.

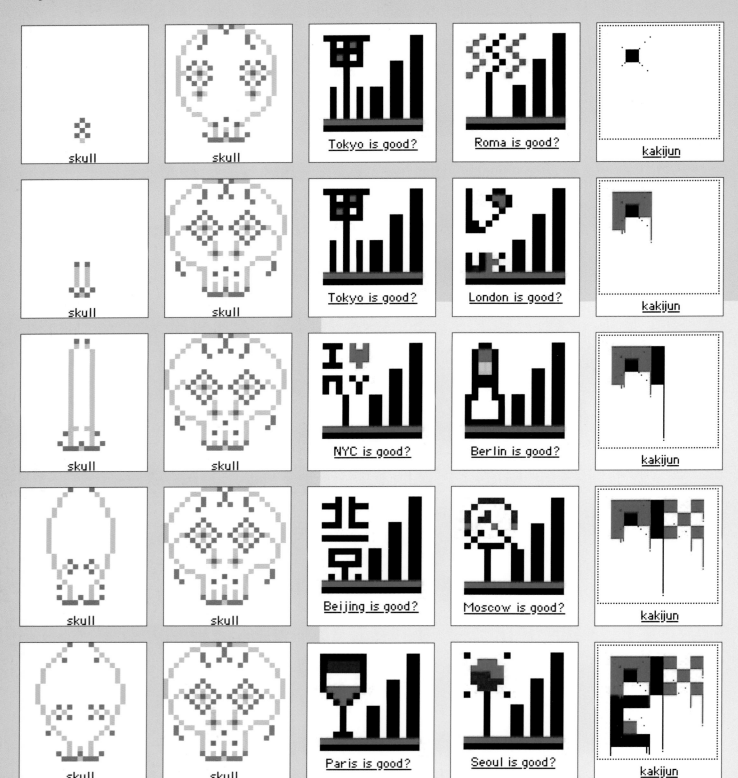

skull

skull

Tokyo is good?

Roma is good?

kakijun

skull

skull

Tokyo is good?

London is good?

kakijun

skull

skull

NYC is good?

Berlin is good?

kakijun

skull

skull

Beijing is good?

Moscow is good?

kakijun

skull

skull

Paris is good?

Seoul is good?

kakijun

TITLE ANIMATIONS · **FORMAT** MOBILE-PHONE
SCREEN ANIMATIONS · **ORIGIN** JAPAN ·
CLIENT MTV MOBILE · **ART DIRECTOR,**
DESIGNER TEN_DO_TEN

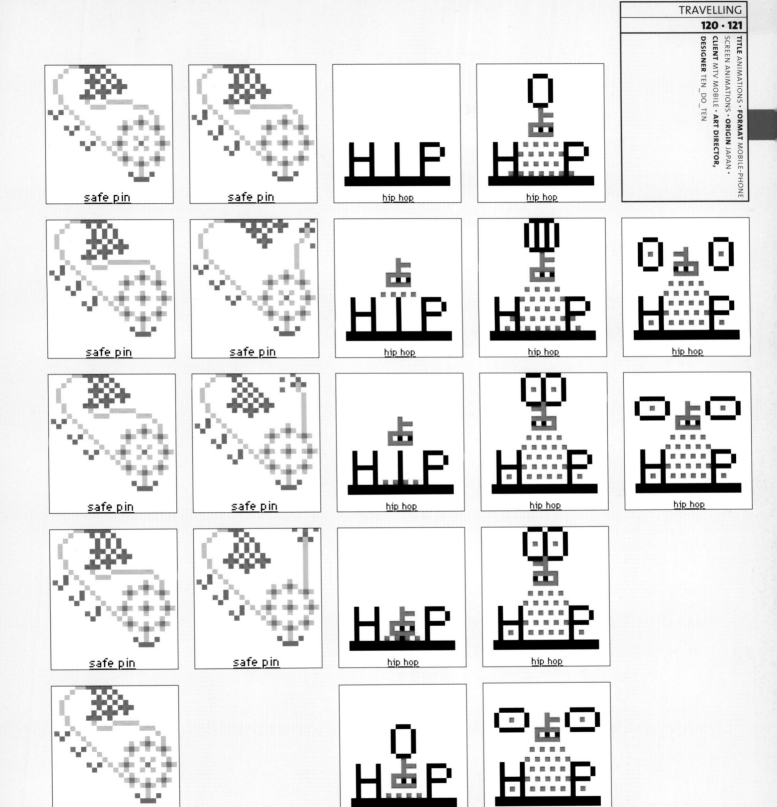

safe pin

safe pin

hip hop

hip hop

safe pin

safe pin

hip hop

hip hop

hip hop

safe pin

safe pin

hip hop

hip hop

hip hop

safe pin

safe pin

hip hop

hip hop

safe pin

hip hop

hip hop

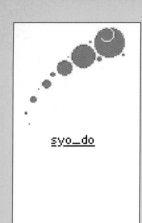

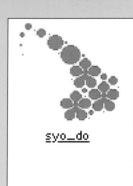

syo_do

syo_do

syo_do

syo_do

Morris skulls

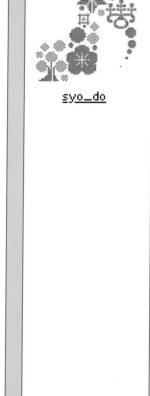

syo_do

syo_do

syo_do

syo_do

Ten design new mobile-phone
screen animations each
week to feature on 'The End',
a section of Tachibana Hajime
Design's website.

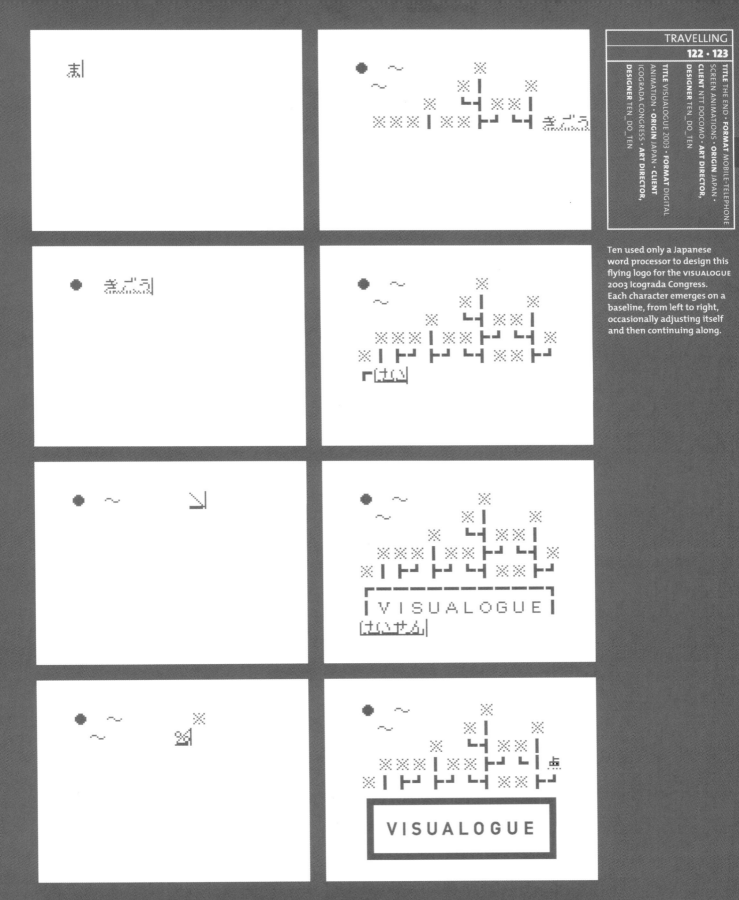

TITLE THE END · FORMAT MOBILE-TELEPHONE
SCREEN ANIMATIONS · ORIGIN JAPAN ·
CLIENT NTT DOCOMO · ART DIRECTOR,
DESIGNER TEN_DO_TEN

TITLE VISUALOGUE 2003 · FORMAT DIGITAL
ANIMATION · ORIGIN JAPAN · CLIENT
ICOGRADA CONGRESS · ART DIRECTOR,
DESIGNER TEN_DO_TEN

Ten used only a Japanese
word processor to design this
flying logo for the VISUALOGUE
2003 Icograda Congress.
Each character emerges on a
baseline, from left to right,
occasionally adjusting itself
and then continuing along.

Automobile Telematics

Fitch is an interdisciplinary design company with twenty-one offices in twelve countries, operating in Asia Pacific, Europe and North America. It specializes in brand consultancy, brand communications, environments, interaction design, product development, packaging and live events. Steve Simula, director of interactive design for Fitch in Columbus, Ohio, developed this prototype automobile telematics system for Nissan.

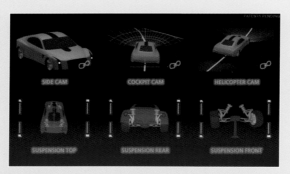

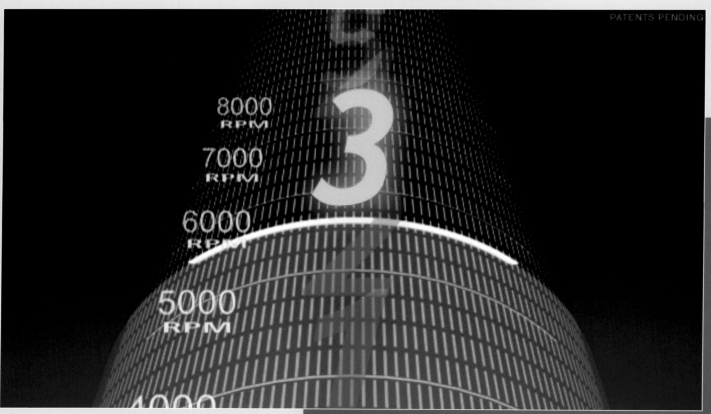

Steve Simula and his team were given the task of designing an interface that would extend the brand identity of Nissan's mm.e concept car.

They wanted to eliminate driver distraction, re-think the car's control board and make it more usable – not just a screen tacked onto the dashboard.

TITLE MM.E AND GT-R CONCEPT CARS ·
FORMAT DASHBOARD INTERFACE · ORIGIN
USA · CLIENT NISSAN · CREATIVE DIRECTOR,
DESIGNER, PRODUCTION STEVE SIMULA

They used technology to enhance the experience that we are used to – letting the car adapt to the driver's needs, not other way around. Features include a GPS unit, elementary voice recognition, and text-to-speech capability to assist drivers with everything from directions to restaurant reservations. The driver can use a mobile phone or on-board computing systems to send and receive e-mail, download music, play movies, obtain driving instructions and browse movie listings while in the car.

For Simula, this does not mean just attaching portable devices to the dashboard but distributing data throughout the car's interior without overwhelming the driver. Observing how video-game designers focus on usability and creating immersive experiences, Simula's team was influenced by *Gran Turismo* by Sony Playstation. For the GT-R concept car, Simula took the standard dashboard RPM and tacheometer displays and – using a video game-style interface – found a way to make drivers feel more connected to their vehicles. Animated digital display gives the driver predictive information, such as when to shift up or down, which enhances safety. A visual representation of what the car is doing helps the driver learn how to drive better and have more confidence on the road.

As a result of Simula's work, the designers of *Gran Turismo* are interested in applying some of his design ideas to their video game.

Soul Hunting

Designer Guido Alvarez feels that he experiences mania – defined as an excessively intense enthusiasm, interest or desire – on a daily basis, and he cures this by making photographs. He sees photographs as flat, airless 'fish tanks' where time stands still. The creatures captured inside the tanks resurrect every time we look at them to remind us of a sensation or a feeling we once experienced and now cherish. Alvarez's thesis project at Virginia Commonwealth University attempted to show the energy captured in his photographic archives as a journey through his memories and imagination, using an experimental interactive method that allows the images to serve as symbols, much like typographic characters, text and phrases can.

Alvarez created nine linked, interactive 'fish tanks', each addressing a category that represents a major aspect of his life. Each is also a representation of a myth, identified by a unique icon. They are stitched together to form Alvarez's pixel-persona for others to visit and experience. The visitor uses the computer mouse to travel within each tank and through icon portals into other tanks.

The first tank contains a series of self-portraits, which are an attempt for Alvarez to know himself better, inspired by the idea that we live in a world where we know our likeness through image, reflection and reproduction only.

The second tank is filled with modern, wingless angels. Alvarez views angels as a hybrid between birds and humans. After a long search for real angels in his home town, Alvarez developed the idea that angels are everywhere, defying gravity by using ladders as wings.

As a response to his idea that angels are everywhere, the third tank portrays fallen (ladderless) angels, who are sitting on sidewalks, in churches and in restaurant entrances. They are found riding on 'homwheels' – the result of interbreeding chairs with bicycles. These angels decide to appear in our dimension and are perceived by society as street beggars. They come in all shapes, sizes, ages and colours, and they are silent and frozen until someone passes by.

The seventh tank relates to worship and belief. It contains human-made objects and scenes that represent God. This tank is a warm-up for the afterlife.

TITLE *SOULHUNTING* · FORMAT DIGITAL INTERACTIVE APPLICATION · ORIGIN USA · DESIGNER, PRODUCTION, AUDIO GUIDO ALVAREZ

The fourth tank contains images of not-so-stereotypical professions in answer to the question: 'When you DON'T grow up, what do you want to be?'

Responding to the notion that we hardly ever realize the value of life until we see death, the eighth tank contains images of death – images without a soul – allowing us to contemplate our own energy. This tank traps death within life and serves as a path to the final tank.

Images of people Alvarez has taught – trapped images of his students – appear in the fifth tank. Each image has been given a place and size according to how much energy he received from that person. They continuously provide Alvarez with the inspiration to work, breathe and design.

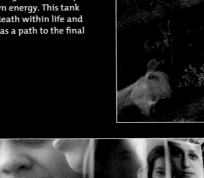

The sixth tank reflects the idea of the 'Venus of Valdivia', a female fertility totem. This sculptural form is part of the first ceramic culture of the Americas, which developed in Ecuador. Each image in this tank has been chosen for possessing an appropriate balance, creating a direct connection with the Venus of Valdivia. This tank has been designed for the visitor to rest, relax and enjoy the 'beautyscape'.

This is Alvarez's final tank, which contains just one photo, a single image that represents the way Alvarez sees God and Her ways.

[god]

Scenting Freedom

Inspired by his thesis project (previous page) Alvarez based *Fishtank Freedom* on the idea that from the very minute we are born we learn to sense the walls that define our freedom. We cannot sense freedom itself, yet we are constantly searching for the experience of it. This project conveys this message in a design for a digital interactive children's book.

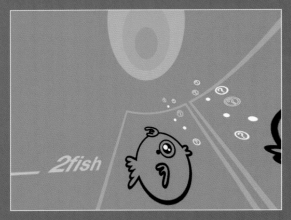

This digital interactive book tells the story of a group of fish who suddenly notice the presence of their invisible confinement and strive to break free by travelling to other fish tanks. As the story unfolds they discover that their tanks have not disappeared but have grown, making the desire for freedom more intense. Their discovery becomes a pledge to share the 'scent of freedom' with the world.

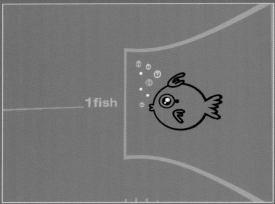

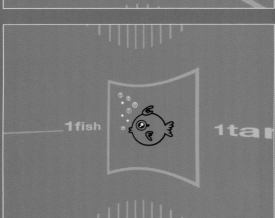

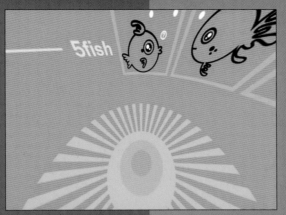

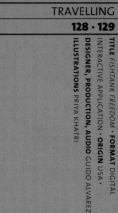

The visitor enters the story near a single fish tank. By using the mouse, the visitor travels around this tank and meet its sole inhabitant: one fish. As the visitor gains familiarity with the surroundings, he or she discovers that there are access ports to more tanks, with more inhabitants. Before long, the visitor has travelled to many tanks, but soon realizes that each fish is trapped in its own tank, even though the tanks are grouped together. The end result is the one-by-one freeing of the fish to join them together in one space without boundaries.

TITLE FISHTANK FREEDOM · FORMAT DIGITAL INTERACTIVE APPLICATION · ORIGIN USA · DESIGNER, PRODUCTION, AUDIO GUIDO ALVAREZ ILLUSTRATIONS PRIYA KHATRI

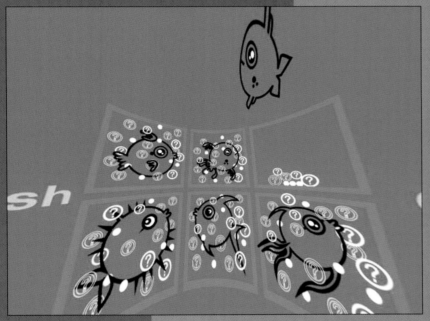

Literary Threads

W. Bradford Paley uses computers to create
readable, clear and engaging visual displays
of complex data. He created his first computer
graphics in 1973, founded Digital Image Design
Incorporated in 1982 and started producing
financial and statistical data visualization in 1986,
some of which are used by brokers on the floor
of the New York Stock Exchange. He has received
multiple grants and awards for both art and
design, and he is adjunct associate professor at
Columbia University, and director of Information
Esthetics, a fledgling interdisciplinary group
that explores the creation and interpretation of
data representations that are both readable and
visually satisfying.

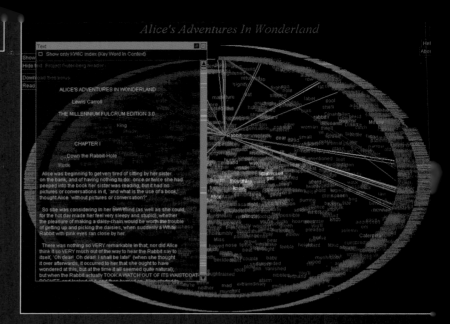

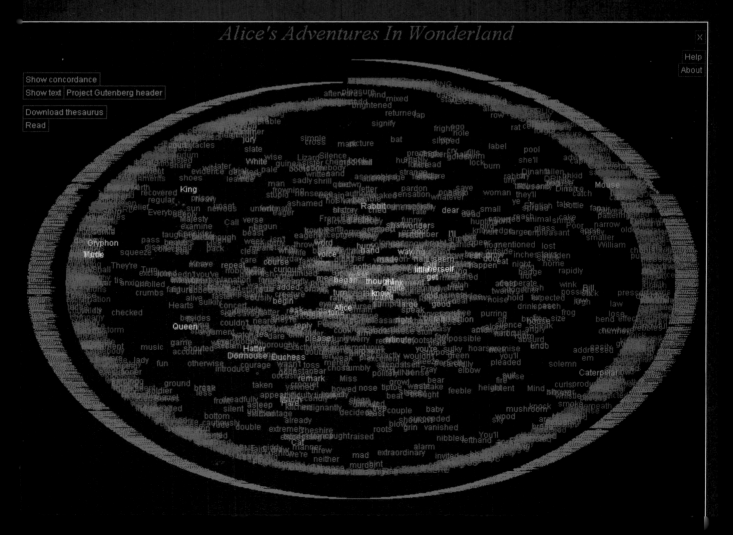

TextArc lays out an entire text – *Alice's Adventures in Wonderland* in this case – twice, to form two concentric circles, starting at the top and proceeding clockwise. Each line is written around the outside circle; every word around the inside, although any word used more than once in the text appears only once on the inside, at its 'average' position. A word mentioned several times moves inward, as if pulled towards each place it is mentioned in the text on the outer circle equally. Thus Alice appears near the middle since she is mentioned all through the book; Rabbit appears closer to the top, since he is mentioned more often at the beginning and end; and Mouse appears close to the outer text since it is mentioned almost exclusively in the Mouse's Chapter, one-fifth of the way into the book. Words that appear more often are brighter. Below is the TextArc for *Alice's Adventures in Wonderland* with lines drawn from the word 'Alice' in the centre to everywhere it appears in the outer text. Bottom, a curved line connects a sequence of words in the order they appear in the text.

TITLE *TEXTARC* · FORMAT INTERACTIVE JAVA APPLICATION, LARGE-FORMAT PRINTS · ORIGIN USA · CREATIVE DESIGNER, PROGRAMMER, PRODUCTION W. BRADFORD PALEY · WEBSITE HTTP://TEXTARC.ORG

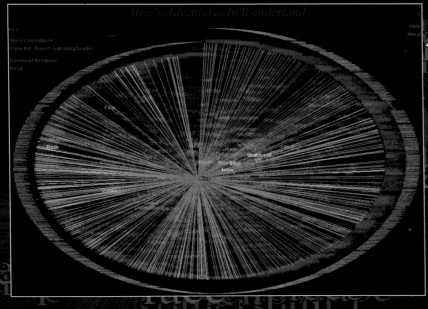

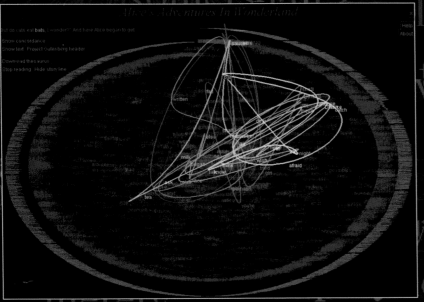

Unravelling the Code

The Whitney Museum commissioned pieces for their 'CODeDOC' exhibition, in which curator Christiane Paul focused on the processes behind computer-based art. Artists were asked to 'connect and move three points in space'. In CodeProfiles, Paley interpreted this brief to connect points within the code itself. Looking at the computer program as written text, he connected points in it in three ways: how code is written by programmers, read by people and executed by computers.

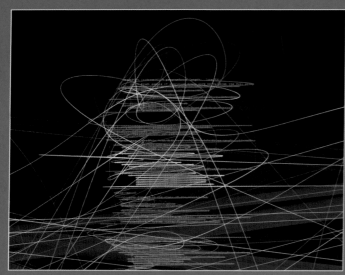

The written code appears in columns, and coloured lines trace these three interpretations of the code, binding it together. A white line traces the programmer's insertion point – the lightest scribbles toward the centre-right show where the most recent code was added. An amber line simulates where the eye might flow as it reads it as columns of text. And a green line follows the execution point of the program, showing code that the computer executed over and over again, overlapping to make wide swaths of light. Each line has its own dynamic character: the green execution point jumps jaggedly from line to line; the white insertion point flows like the programmer's thoughts, character by character; and the amber fixation point plods along, reading every word with bookish rigour.

The interactive version of CodeProfiles is a custom-built computer with an oversized touch screen. Stroking a line magnifies it to a readable size and tapping it restarts all three traces at that point.

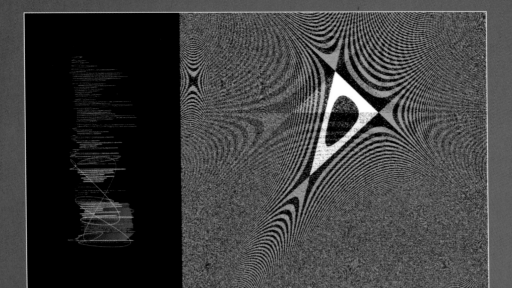

TITLE CODEPROFILES · FORMAT INTERACTIVE JAVA APPLICATION,
LARGE-FORMAT PRINTS · ORIGIN USA · CLIENT CHRISTIANE PAUL,
WHITNEY MUSEUM OF AMERICAN ART · CREATIVE DESIGNER,
PROGRAMMER, PRODUCTION W. BRADFORD PALEY · 'ACCIDENTAL'
COLLABORATORS SCOTT SNIBBE, MARTIN WATTENBERG

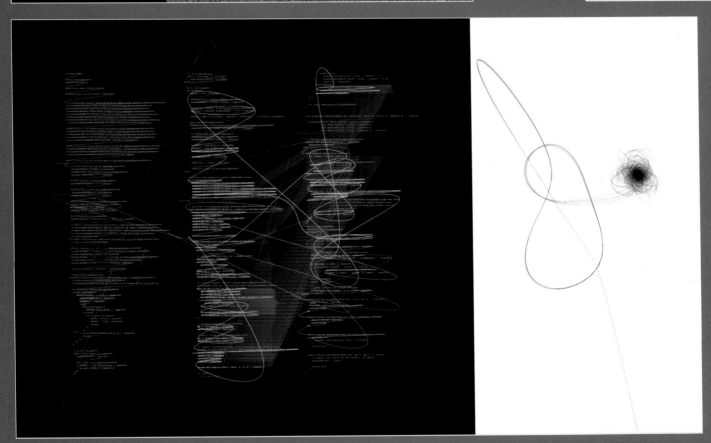

Paley also applied CodeProfiles to two other artists' codes. Martin Wattenberg's ConnectApplet (top) produces a shimmering moiré pattern by applying a mathematical function to a triangle as the points are dragged and moved. His code is tiny since the visual structure all comes from this single function. And the tight inner loop – painting each point black, white or grey – is tinier still.

Scott Snibbe's work TriPolar (above) shows how a pendulum moves above three magnets (its output is on the right). The often-repeated green inner loop, centre and right, does most of the work.

Playing with Time

Yugo Nakamura is a designer and engineer who explores interactive systems in digital and networked environments. He has shown work at the Centre Pompidou in Paris, the Kunstlerhaus in Vienna and the Design Museum in London and he has received awards from Cannes Lions, OneShow, Clio Award and ADC NY. In these projects from his website, which he updates and archives meticulously, he has adapted his architectural and engineering training to work in digital typography, creating a new dimension for navigating and reading information. Through complex coding, visitor's to his website can bring typography to life.

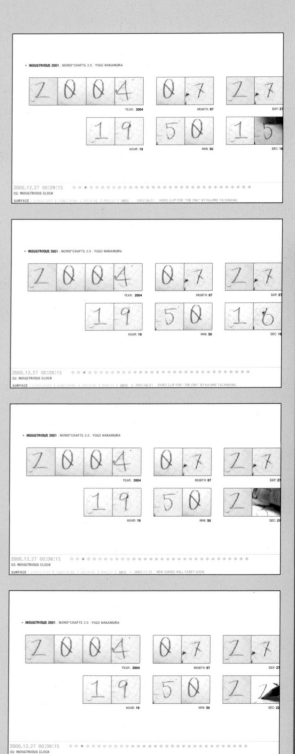

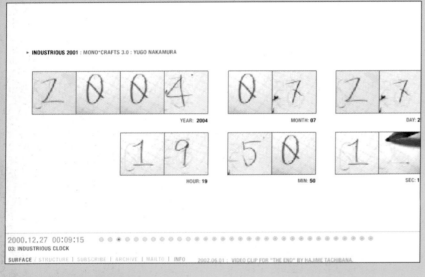

Nakamura's *Industrious Clock* application uses dynamic data by tapping into the time and date setting of the user's computer. The data is shown in the form of numerals hand-drawn on paper and stored as characters. The cycle of numerals through year, month, day, hour, minute and second is indicated by a human hand erasing a character and writing a new one in its place. This process is accelerated to be consistent with the speed of changing seconds.

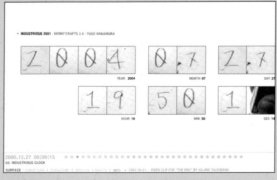

Year of the Snake also taps into the clock and date data on the user's computer. The only information that does not change is the year he identifies as the first of the new millennium: 2001. The information is revealed as the user moves the mouse around the viewing frame. The time and date repeat in a three-

– that loops in circles and curves in the space.

TRAVELLING

134 · 135

TITLE *INDUSTRIOUS CLOCK* · **FORMAT** DIGITAL INTERACTIVE ANIMATION · **ORIGIN** JAPAN · **DESIGNER, PROGRAMMER** YUGO NAKAMURA

TITLE *YEAR OF THE SNAKE* · **FORMAT** DIGITAL INTERACTIVE ANIMATION · **ORIGIN** JAPAN · **CLIENT** MR & MRS TAMAMORI, ©2001 SHORT CUT, LTD. · **DESIGNER, PROGRAMMER** YUGO NAKAMURA

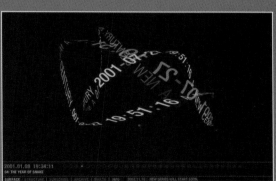

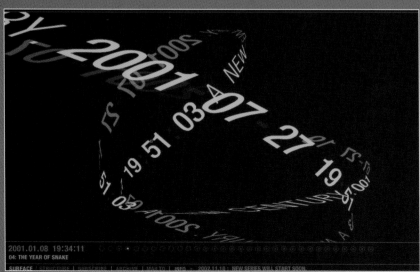

The words in the piece *Rigid Body 01* move according to rigid body dynamics; when clicked on the user may 'throw' the heavyweight 'one', 'two' and 'three'. The words exhibit the inertia characteristic of solid objects as they travel across the viewing frame and eventually come to a stop, suspended in space.

2001.11.05 09:10:30 ● ○ ○ ○ ○ ○ ○ ○ ○ ○ ○ ○ ○
25: RE-ISSUE 02: SHIFT
SURFACE / STRUCTURE | SUBSCRIBE | ARCHIVE | MAILTO | INFO ► 2002.06.01 : VIDEO CLIP FOR "THE END" BY HAJIME TACHIBANA.

This application was created for the cover of online magazine *Shift*. Floating globs of characters fill the space; clicking on any one of them causes the characters to unscramble and form a provocative phrase related to design, music, learning or discovery. A large database allows seemingly endless variation:

> Design is a Message
> Image Co-Evolution
> Nothing but Good Design
> Sound of Silence
> Experience Teaches

TITLE *RIGID BODY 01: DYNAMIC DRAG & THROW* ·
FORMAT DIGITAL INTERACTIVE ANIMATION ·
ORIGIN JAPAN · DESIGNER, PROGRAMMER
YUGO NAKAMURA

TITLE *SHIFT MAGAZINE COVER* · FORMAT DIGITAL
INTERACTIVE ANIMATION · ORIGIN JAPAN · CLIENT
SHIFT MAGAZINE · DESIGNERS, PROGRAMMERS
SHINZO, KAZSH, KURI, YUGO NAKAMURA

2001.11.05 09:10:30 ● ● ● ● ● ● ● ● ● ● ● ● ○ ● ● ●
25: RE-ISSUE 02: SHIFT
SURFACE / STRUCTURE | SUBSCRIBE | ARCHIVE | MAILTO | INFO ► 2002.11.10 : NEW SERIES WILL START SOON.

you d ... you want

2001.11.05 09:10:30 ● ● ● ● ● ● ● ● ● ● ● ● ● ● ●
25: RE-ISSUE 02: SHIFT
SURFACE / STRUCTURE | SUBSCRIBE | ARCHIVE | MAILTO | INFO ► 2002.06.01 : VIDEO CLIP FOR "THE END" BY HAJIME TACHIBANA.

no nad e f

2001.11.05 09:10:30 ● ● ● ● ● ● ● ● ● ● ● ● ● ○ ● ●
25: RE-ISSUE 02: SHIFT
SURFACE / STRUCTURE | SUBSCRIBE | ARCHIVE | MAILTO | INFO ► 2002.11.10 : NEW SERIES WILL START SOON.

2001.11.05 09:10:30 ● ● ● ● ● ● ● ● ● ● ● ● ● ○ ● ●
25: RE-ISSUE 02: SHIFT
SURFACE / STRUCTURE | SUBSCRIBE | ARCHIVE | MAILTO | INFO ► 2002.11.10 : NEW SERIES WILL START SOON.

now and forever

2001.11.05 09:10:30 ● ● ● ● ● ● ● ● ● ● ● ● ● ○ ● ●
25: RE-ISSUE 02: SHIFT
SURFACE / STRUCTURE | SUBSCRIBE | ARCHIVE | MAILTO | INFO ► 2002.06.01 : VIDEO CLIP FOR "THE END" BY HAJIME TACHIBANA.

2001.11.05 09:10:30 ● ● ● ● ● ● ● ● ● ● ● ● ● ○ ○ ○
25: RE-ISSUE 02: SHIFT
SURFACE / STRUCTURE | SUBSCRIBE | ARCHIVE | MAILTO | INFO 2002.11.10 : NEW SERIES WILL START SOON.

Nakamura created this interface application for Sony that works with the computer keyboard. The twenty-six letters of the alphabet are suspended in a group. Typing one letter causes it to pulsate on screen and a colour-coded circular force field emerges from the letter, pushing all the others away. Releasing the key turns off the field and the letters resume their position in the group. Typing many keys rapidly creates a chaotic eruption of pulses and force fields, and the letters scatter around the entire viewing frame.

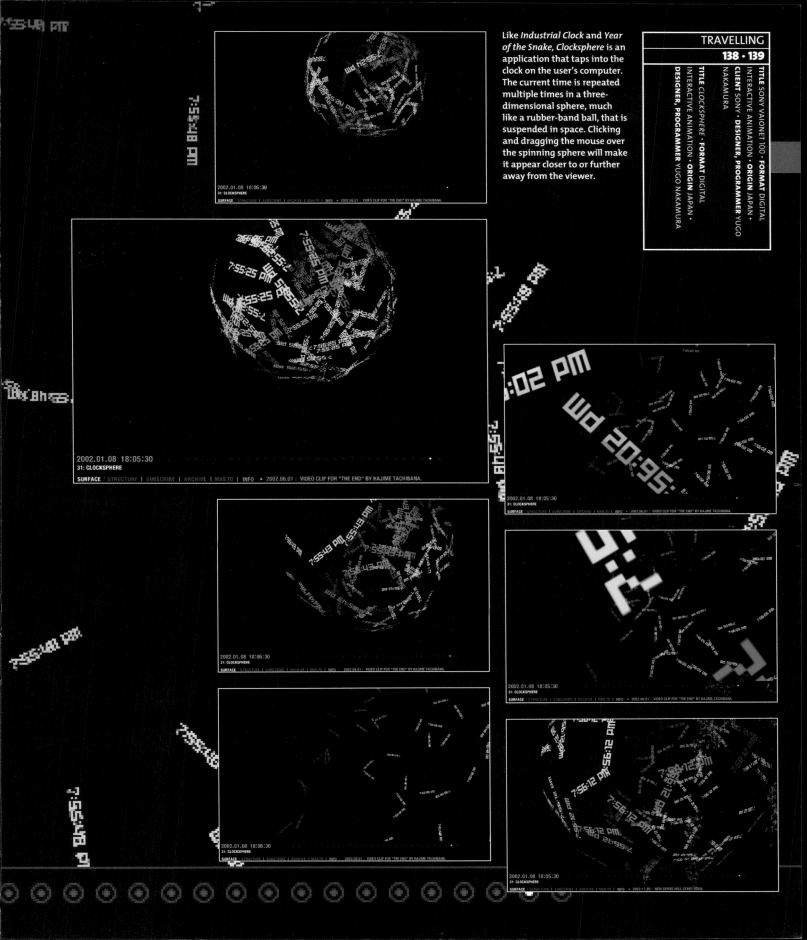

Like *Industrial Clock* and *Year of the Snake, Clocksphere* is an application that taps into the clock on the user's computer. The current time is repeated multiple times in a three-dimensional sphere, much like a rubber-band ball, that is suspended in space. Clicking and dragging the mouse over the spinning sphere will make it appear closer to or further away from the viewer.

TITLE SONY VAIONET 100 · **FORMAT** DIGITAL

INTERACTIVE ANIMATION · **ORIGIN** JAPAN ·

CLIENT SONY · **DESIGNER, PROGRAMMER** YUGO

NAKAMURA

TITLE *CLOCKSPHERE* · **FORMAT** DIGITAL

INTERACTIVE ANIMATION · **ORIGIN** JAPAN ·

DESIGNER, PROGRAMMER YUGO NAKAMURA

2002.01.08 18:05:30
31: CLOCKSPHERE
SURFACE / STRUCTURE | SUBSCRIBE | ARCHIVE | MAILTO | INFO ► 2002.06.01 : VIDEO CLIP FOR "THE END" BY HAJIME TACHIBANA.

TITLE *THE RETAIL EXPERIMENT* · **FORMAT**
INTERACTIVE VIDEO INSTALLATION · **ORIGIN**
USA · **CLIENT** DIESEL DENIM GALLERY ·
DESIGNER, PRODUCTION TRONIC STUDIO

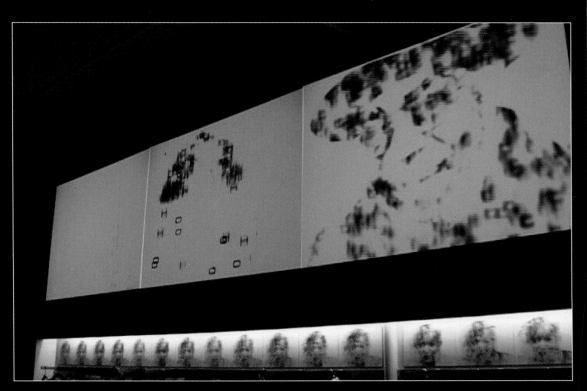

The Retail Experiment is an interactive video installation created by Tronic Studio (see p. 28) for the Diesel Denim Gallery in New York. The studio filmed interviews with over a hundred people of different ages, asking them to recall one of their fondest memories. A morphing process shows these people becoming younger and younger as they recount their memories.

To further engage the visitor, Tronic Studio designed an ATM-like booth that captured a visitor's photo as they entered the exhibit. Then, in real time, the image was incorporated into the video projections and became part of the cycle.

Tronic Studio was the main design studio for Nextfest, a three-day technology fair hosted by *Wired* magazine. The studio was involved in every aspect of the physical exhibition space – architecture, motion graphics, signage – and the website (www.nextfest.net).

THE FUTURE OF
HEALTH

THE FUTURE OF
TRANSPORTATION

THE FUTURE OF
HEALTH

THE FUTURE OF
TRANSPORTATION

Atmospheric Type

TITLE NEXTFEST · **FORMAT** ARCHITECTURE/
TITLE DESIGN/BRANDING/INTERACTIVE
DESIGN · **ORIGIN** USA · **CLIENT** WIRED ·
ART DIRECTORS REI INAMOTO, VIVIAN
ROSENTHAL, JESSE SEPPI · **ARCHITECTURAL
CONSULTANTS** ADAM DAYEM, AHM
CHANDAWANICH · **TITLES, BRANDING,
INTERACTIVE CONSULTANTS** MARLON
HERNANDEZ, GARRY WALLER · **MUSIC**
COMBUSTION

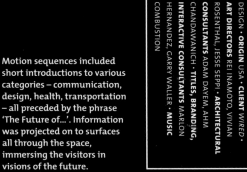

Motion sequences included
short introductions to various
categories – communication,
design, health, transportation
– all preceded by the phrase
'The Future of...'. Information
was projected on to surfaces
all through the space,
immersing the visitors in
visions of the future.

Architext

In the conservative German-speaking Swiss capital Bern, the cutting-edge design of BüroDestruct seems out of place. In fact, the very name of the studio, founded in 1992, is contradictory. A 'Büro' is an office, a place of orderly and careful behaviour, while 'Destruct' suggests devastation and change. BüroDestruct's work features tortured, distorted three-dimensional imagery and aggressive typography, which pays homage to Swiss graphic legend Josef Müller-Brockmann. The firm maintains its fresh visual language by keeping up to date with music and club scenes and taking in the environments they visit around the world.

Typotown is a small application that makes it possible to build cities out of fonts. BüroDestruct came up with the idea after trips to various cities where they saw many beautiful typefaces and letters mounted on walls and on signs on buildings.

In Typotown the characters become the architecture: the user may change the typeface and enter text to create the cityscape, customizing the façades by using transparency, outline, light and shadow, colour and tracer. Simple navigational actions are possible, including travelling around and within its streets and flying overhead and underneath the street surface.

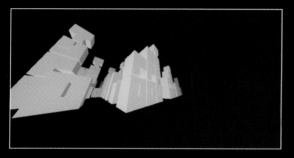

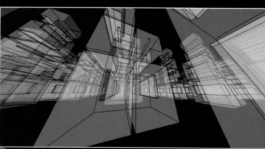

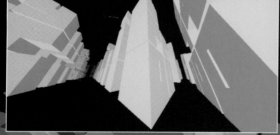

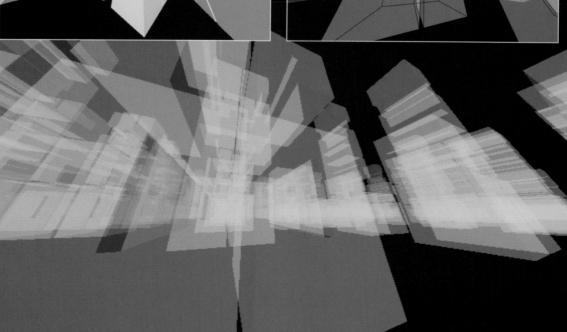

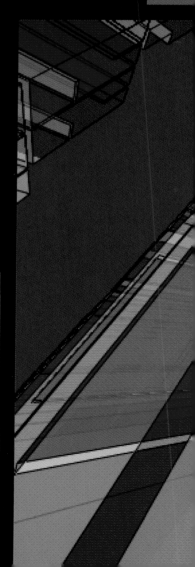

TITLE TYPOTOWN · **FORMAT** DIGITAL
INTERACTIVE APPLICATION · **ORIGIN**
SWITZERLAND · **DESIGNER, PROGRAMMER**
BÜRODESTRUCT
©2002–2003 BÜRODESTRUCT BERN,
SWITZERLAND

Transformative Type

Ben Hannam graduated from Virginia Commonwealth University with an MFA in design and visual communication in 2002. He is a freelance designer and has written and lectured on enhancing visual communication through the manipulation of depth perception and time-based media and currently teaches graphic design at the Virginia Commonwealth University in Qatar. Hannam designed the website for 'Tasmeem Doha', an annual design conference held in Qatar (*tasmeem* is Arabic for design). The conference's aim is to establish discussions within the design community and to provide examples of how the design process, practice and application can be a vital resource for a healthy and changing society in the Middle East.

Information on the website needed to be available in Arabic and English. Hannam wanted the design to emphasize the two languages equally, so the Arabic and English information mirror each other and a splash page allows the user to pick their preferred language.

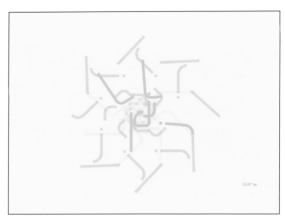

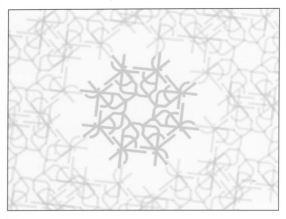

Peter Martin, conference Chair and colleague at VCU in Qatar, helped Hannam create the typographic animation that reinforces the conference identity, immerses the user and takes them to the home page. Martin created the typography from modules derived from Islamic patterns. These modules were adapted as part of the conference aesthetic and were used as graphics in the print campaign.

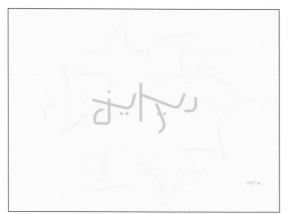

TITLE TASMEEM DOHA · **FORMAT** WEB SITE SPLASH/INTRODUCTION AND INTERFACE · **ORIGIN** QATAR · **DESIGNERS, PROGRAMMERS** BEN HANNAM, PETER MARTIN

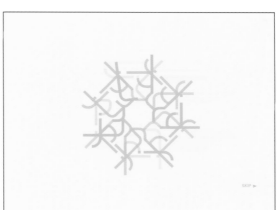

Once users have been redirected to the home page in their language of choice, they use the Islamic patterns as a means of navigating the site. To present the patterning in a three-dimensional format Hannam skewed it to appear as if it had a vanishing point in the distance. The pattern rotates slowly on an axis and has a roll-over function that reveals the various options before the visitor clicks on the link.

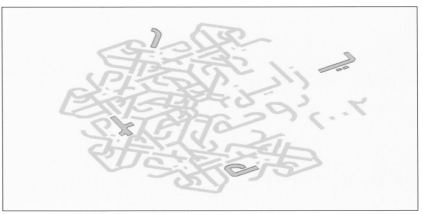

Mobile Ideography

Kyle Barrow is a mobile web evangelist and designer based in Osaka, Japan. His web site, pukupi.com, contains articles, a blog, tools and resources for designing web pages for mobile phones. Within his resources section is a catalogue of *emoji*, the Japanese ideographs for mobile telephones. *Emoji* are largely the creation of mobile carriers – au, DoCoMo, Vodafone – and each carrier has its own set of *emoji* and uses a different method for displaying them. *Emoji* have travelled as far as Europe with their meaning largely intact but with different, incompatible, codes to the Japanese ones. Pukupi's *emoji* resource aims to reconcile these differences.

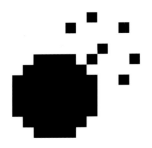

TRAVELLING

148 · 149

TITLE *EMOJI* · **FORMAT** MOBILE
TELEPHONE IDEOGRAPHS · **ORIGIN**
EUROPE AND JAPAN · **DESIGNERS**
VARIOUS TELEPHONE CARRIERS

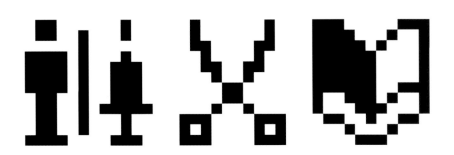

Graffiti in Motion

PIPS:lab is an Amsterdam-based multidisciplinary art collective comprising a photographer, an inventor, a composer, a playwright, an illustrator, a musician and a music producer/DJ. Combining film, photography and interaction, PIPS:lab has developed several innovative cameras, photographic techniques and new ways of enabling interaction.

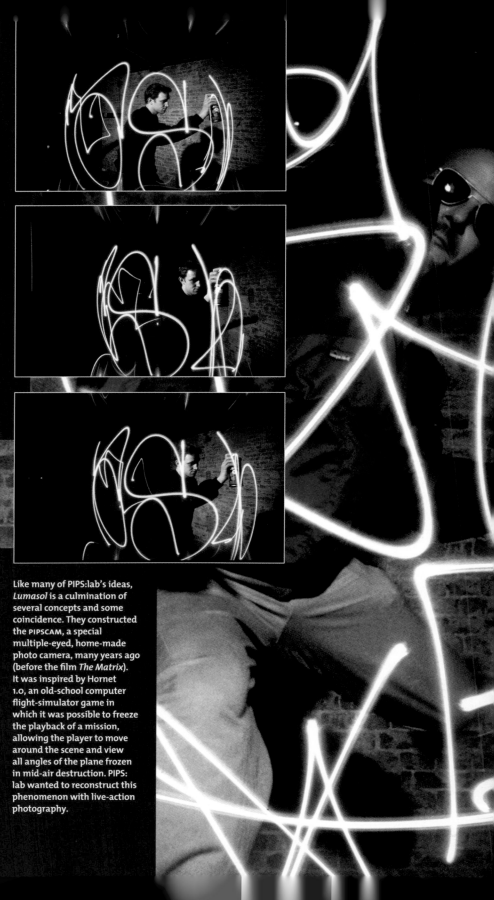

Like many of PIPS:lab's ideas, *Lumasol* is a culmination of several concepts and some coincidence. They constructed the PIPSCAM, a special multiple-eyed, home-made photo camera, many years ago (before the film *The Matrix*). It was inspired by Hornet 1.0, an old-school computer flight-simulator game in which it was possible to freeze the playback of a mission, allowing the player to move around the scene and view all angles of the plane frozen in mid-air destruction. PIPS:lab wanted to reconstruct this phenomenon with live-action photography.

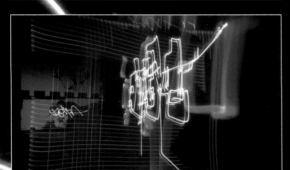

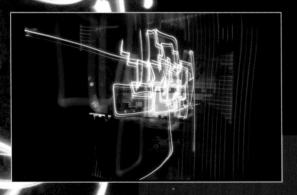

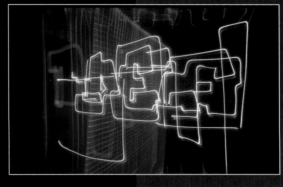

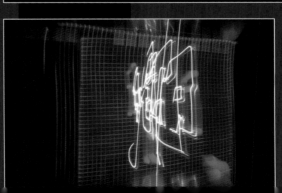

130 • 131

TITLE *LUMASOL* • FORMAT LIGHT
GRAFFITI• ORIGIN THE NETHERLANDS •
ARTISTS (LEFT TO RIGHT) CRASH2, KRAZE,
DELTA • DIRECTORS KEEZ DUVVES, REMCO
VERVEER • PHOTOGRAPHY PIPS:LAB •
PRODUCTION KEEZ DUVVES, REMCO
VERVEER

Post-production was
incredibly time-consuming:
fifty negatives per shot had
to be scanned and centred
to generate just a few
enlightening seconds
of footage.

It came together when the
group created a piece in
collaboration with MODE2
– a well-known Parisian
graffiti artist – for the
clothing company Carhartt,
for which PIPS:lab invented
the three-dimensional
Lumasol technique. They
set up a system of multiple
cameras (which they call PIPS
photographic interactive
parallel sequence) to capture
the artist writing a 'piece' with
an empty spraycan, which
had a light bulb attached to it.
Placed in a sequence, this light
painting became a virtual
three-dimensional object.

As well as PIPS:lab, many
graffiti artists and illustrators
were involved. The artists
worked in complete darkness
and were also working in
three dimensions, when they
were used to painting on two-
dimensional surfaces.

05   Speculating

This chapter includes a wide variety of activity that arises out of pure experimentation at the cutting edge of type and lettering design in time-based media. The primary goal is the manipulation of binary code to realize new ideas, functions and methods of communication with type and lettering. Some of these projects are examples of data-driven design, using a data source and a computer algorithm to generate what appears on screen, rather than the designer's eye.

Typographic Organisms

Typorganism is a thesis project created by Gicheol Lee for the MFA degree in computer art at the School of Visual Arts, New York. It is a web-based project composed of eight communication experiments that focus on interactive kinetic typography in a web environment. Lee used the metaphor of type as an organism with the aim of demonstrating five characteristics of interactive web-based typography that explain this metaphor. These were: evolution, (type evolving through time); dynamism (dynamic movement and content); intelligence (designed using software algorithms); responsiveness (responsive to the user's stimulus); and propagation (propagates through a network).

Lee shows recent programming techniques can alter typography in the web environment. Influenced by John Maeda, John Simon Jr, Mark Napier and Yugo Nakamura (see p. 134), Lee's research concentrated on developing the Internet as a design resource. The metaphor of living organisms also suggested issues raised by scientific achievements such as the Human Genome project.

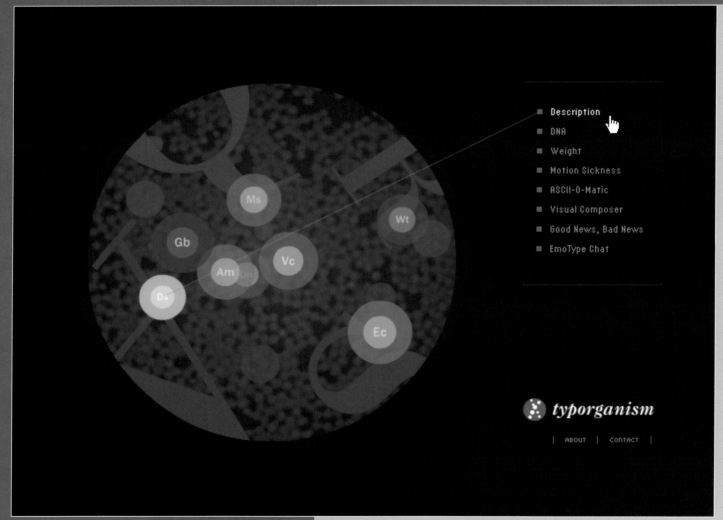

TITLE *TYPORGANISM* · **FORMAT** DIGITAL INTERACTIVE WEB APPLICATIONS · **ORIGIN** USA · **DESIGNER, PROGRAMMER** GICHEOL LEE

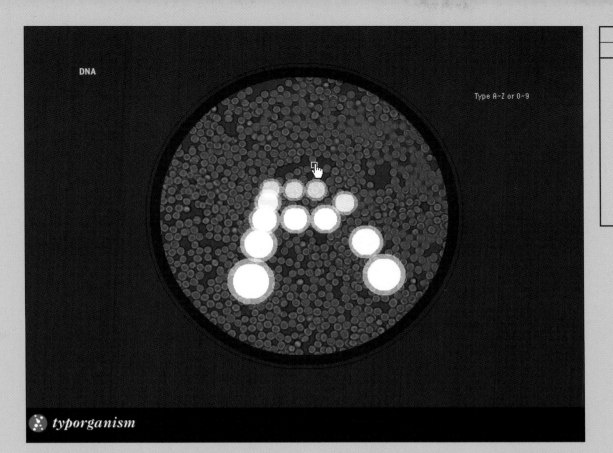

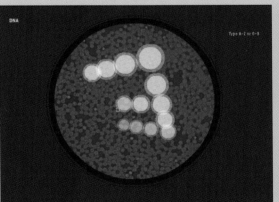
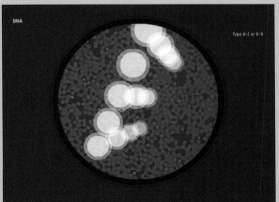
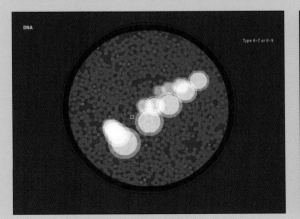
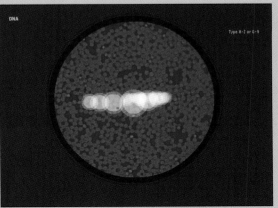

Since 1999, Lee has been applying maths and physics formulas to his experiments in motion design. Lee thought that if he could compose a list of commands and apply them to a visual element, its behaviour may mimic that of a small life form by reacting to instructions. The movements are determined by a software algorithm.

In *DNA* letters are formed from molecular elements in a petri dish. The user enters a letter or numeral on the keyboard to generate it in the dish, then slides the small yellow square around the dish with the mouse to 'inspect' the creation in multiple dimensions.

ASCII Image

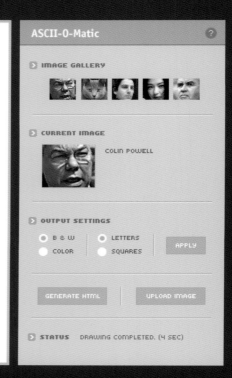

 typorganism

ASCII-O-Matic is a web application by Lee that converts images into ASCII art automatically. Users can upload an image from their hard drive and then view the ASCII art image generated by the software. They can even open up an HTML version of ASCII art and copy the HTML source code to use it on their own website. This is a good example of 'text as an image', and it reminds us of the printed ASCII art imagery in the early days of computer graphics.

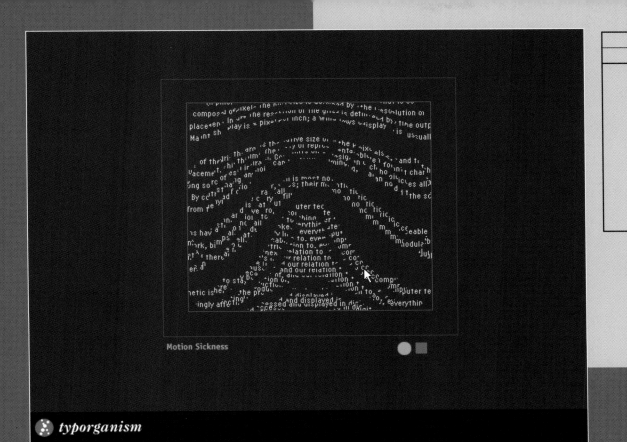

SPECULATING

156 · 157

TITLE *TYPOGRANISM* · **FORMAT** DIGITAL
INTERACTIVE WEB APPLICATIONS · **ORIGIN**
USA · **DESIGNER, PROGRAMMER** GICHEOL LEE

typorganism

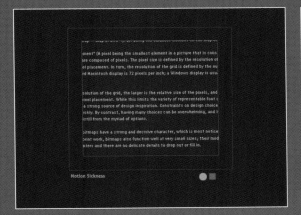

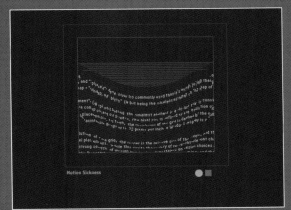

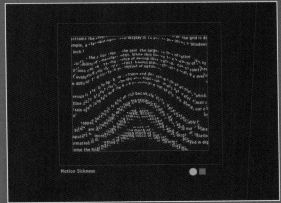

Motion Sickness displays text
innocently within a viewing
frame. However, the line
width extends beyond the
frame, requiring the reader
to use the mouse to scroll over
the text and slide it left, right,
up or down. In doing this the
static, calm plane of text is
disturbed and it ripples and
contorts like water's surface
after a rock has been tossed in,
leaving the reader disoriented.

Tactile Typography

Designer and artist Brian Lemen's MFA thesis project addresses the modular construction of type in pixels on a computer screen and how type can be constructed physically using other materials. It is a prototype system for letterform design and also a means of experimentation and exploration in digital and physical environments; physical exploration with typographic form will lead to a more critical and sensitive understanding of type on the computer screen and vice versa.

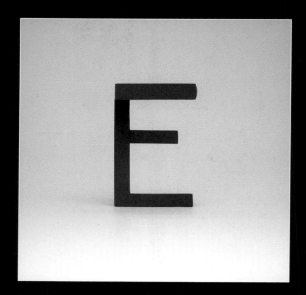

Lemen used the typeface family Verdana for his explorations. Designed by Matthew Carter and hand-tinted by Tom Rickner, Verdana was created with the computer screen in mind. This type family consists of four TrueType fonts that were intended to address common issues and challenges of digitally-displayed type, although the designers felt that Verdana's uses go beyond the screen. They considered its modular construction pixel by pixel, taking into consideration its varying sizes and uses. This is precisely the level of craft and attention to detail that Lemen wished to emphasize.

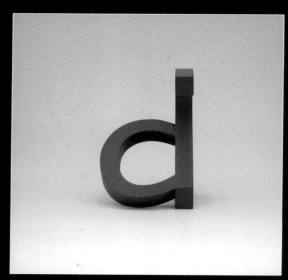

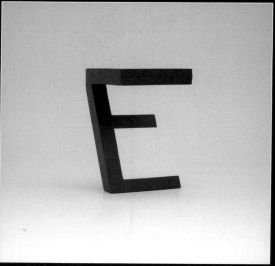

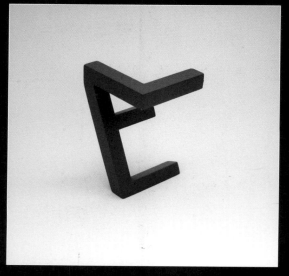

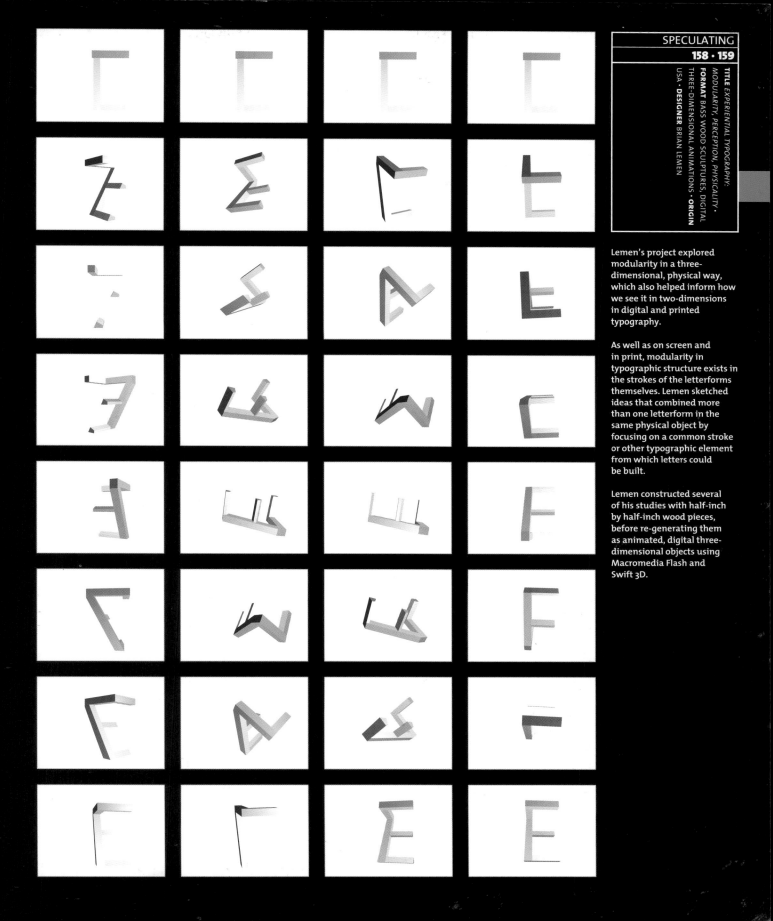

TITLE EXPERIENTIAL TYPOGRAPHY: MODULARITY, PERCEPTION, PHYSICALITY · **FORMAT** BASS WOOD SCULPTURES, DIGITAL THREE-DIMENSIONAL ANIMATIONS · **ORIGIN** USA · **DESIGNER** BRIAN LEMEN

Lemen's project explored modularity in a three-dimensional, physical way, which also helped inform how we see it in two-dimensions in digital and printed typography.

As well as on screen and in print, modularity in typographic structure exists in the strokes of the letterforms themselves. Lemen sketched ideas that combined more than one letterform in the same physical object by focusing on a common stroke or other typographic element from which letters could be built.

Lemen constructed several of his studies with half-inch by half-inch wood pieces, before re-generating them as animated, digital three-dimensional objects using Macromedia Flash and Swift 3D.

Time in Motion

Chisa Yagi is a Japanese-born designer based in New York who develops experimental typography for print and motion. Yagi created the dynamic screen typeface Timeface in the interactive design 2.0 visualization and dynamic data course taught by Eddie Opara and George Plesko at Yale School of Art.

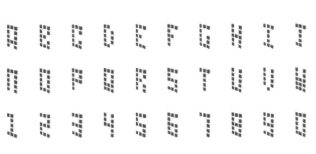

The original two-dimensional typeface is based on fifteen pixels arranged on a three-by-five grid. By placing the bitmap typeface in a virtual three-dimensional environment (right) and rotating each pixel according to an algorithm that takes numerical values from an assigned dynamic data source, Yagi created a continually changing typeface.

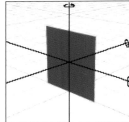

Yagi needed three numeric values to input into the xyz coordinates to move each pixel in three dimensions. She chose time (hour, minute, second) as the data source and used the computer's clock to dynamically change the typeface's appearance as time progresses.

The pixels, therefore, rotate on three axes and more complex rotations occur when more than one variable changes at the same time.

In the sample frames (right), the typeface is linked to the computer's clock, set to the 24-hour format. So that each pixel within a letterform rotated differently, Yagi linked each one to a different time zone. Rolling the mouse over a pixel indicates the city contributing the time data.

TITLE TIMEFACE · FORMAT DYNAMIC
TYPEFACE · ORIGIN USA · ADVISING FACULTY
EDDIE OPARA, GEORGE PLESKO · DESIGNER,
PROGRAMMER CHISA YAGI

I AM A DUMMY COPY

AND I'VE BEEN A DUMMY COPY SINCE MY BIRTH.

IT TOOK ME A LONG TIME TO REALIZE WHAT IT MEANS TO BE A DUMMY COPY. YOU MAKE NO SENSE. YOU STAND OUT NOW AND THEN BY BEING COMPLETELY OUT OF CONTEXT. OFTEN, YOU AREN'T EVEN READ AT ALL. DOES THAT MAKE ME A BAD COPY? I KNOW THAT I'LL NEVER STAND A CHANCE OF APPEARING IN THE ECONOMIST. BUT DOES THAT MAKE ME ANY LESS IMPORTANT? I'M A DUMMY! BUT I ENJOY BEING A COPY. AND SHOULD YOU NOW DECIDE TO CARRY ON READING ME TO THE END, I'LL HAVE MANAGED TO ACHIEVE SOMETHING MOST 'NORMAL' COPIES DON'T ACHIEVE.

Timeface is a study in embedding dynamic data within individual letterforms. When the typeface is printed, the rotation of the pixels becomes the embodiment of one specific time, the time stamp of the moment of input.

I AM A DUMMY COPY

AND I'VE BEEN A DUMMY COPY SINCE MY BIRTH.

IT TOOK ME A LONG TIME TO REALIZE WHAT IT MEANS TO BE A DUMMY COPY. YOU MAKE NO SENSE. YOU STAND OUT NOW AND THEN BY BEING COMPLETELY OUT OF CONTEXT. OFTEN, YOU AREN'T EVEN READ AT ALL. DOES THAT MAKE ME A BAD COPY? I KNOW THAT I'LL NEVER STAND A CHANCE OF APPEARING IN THE ECONOMIST. BUT DOES THAT MAKE ME ANY LESS IMPORTANT? I'M A DUMMY! BUT I ENJOY BEING A COPY. AND SHOULD YOU NOW DECIDE TO CARRY ON READING ME TO THE END, I'LL HAVE MANAGED TO ACHIEVE SOMETHING MOST 'NORMAL' COPIES DON'T ACHIEVE.

Offering some challenges in terms of legibility, the typeface is not very practical, but it creates an intriguing appearance. Yagi believes the typeface truly visualizes dynamic data.

I AM A DUMMY COPY

AND I'VE BEEN A DUMMY COPY SINCE MY BIRTH.

IT TOOK ME A LONG TIME TO REALIZE WHAT IT MEANS TO BE A DUMMY COPY. YOU MAKE NO SENSE. YOU STAND OUT NOW AND THEN BY BEING COMPLETELY OUT OF CONTEXT. OFTEN, YOU AREN'T EVEN READ AT ALL. DOES THAT MAKE ME A BAD COPY? I KNOW THAT I'LL NEVER STAND A CHANCE OF APPEARING IN THE ECONOMIST. BUT DOES THAT MAKE ME ANY LESS IMPORTANT? I'M A DUMMY! BUT I ENJOY BEING A COPY. AND SHOULD YOU NOW DECIDE TO CARRY ON READING ME TO THE END, I'LL HAVE MANAGED TO ACHIEVE SOMETHING MOST 'NORMAL' COPIES DON'T ACHIEVE.

Matt Woolman keeps his closet packed with several hats, many of which he wears simultaneously: Professor, designer, author... and artist. Woolman founded PLAID Studios as an outlet for his many creative activities, including non-commercial, experimental projects such as these.

TITLE *PIXEL AQUARIUMS* · FORMAT ACRYLIC SCULPTURE · ORIGIN USA · ARTIST MATT WOOLMAN

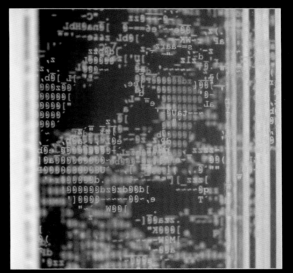

The pixels we view on a computer screen are nothing but tiny squares of light – apparitions that disappear when the computer is turned off. Woolman believes that art must have material value, so these acrylic sculptures explore the concept of material pixels. The boxes, which are similar to fish aquariums, contain pixel forms, but unlike an aquarium or a computer no external power source is required.

The study on the opposite page and left column of this page was the first in a series where Woolman broke down the story, 'Trading Citie 5', from *Invisible Cities*, by Italo Calvino, into primary words (nouns, verbs and adjectives) and secondary words (prepositions, conjunctions and articles). Each set of words was transferred onto a separate transparent acrylic panel. When inserted into the container and observed from various angles as it is rotated, the words synthesize to form other stories.

Similarly, the right column features images created using ASCII characters, which have been transferred to multiple layers of transparent acrylic panels, to give them a sense of depth and three-dimensionality.

Scissors, Paper, Type

Avi Haltovsky's final project for his BFA in communication design, majoring in multimedia design, at Bezalel Academy of Art and Design in Jerusalem was Papercut. Haltovsky is creative director and manager of the promo department at JCS Post Production in Tel Aviv, the leading post-production house in Israel.

Three-dimensional design elements are used frequently in electronic media design, computer games, television advertising and websites, but the fonts employed are outdated and do not utilize the three-dimensional medium to its full potential. There is an obvious need for developments that combine three-dimensional elements into the visual design of the typography.

Instead of taking an existing font and giving it three-dimensional characteristics, Haltovsky based Papercut on a three-dimensional shape, and its motion illustrated how each letter was constructed.

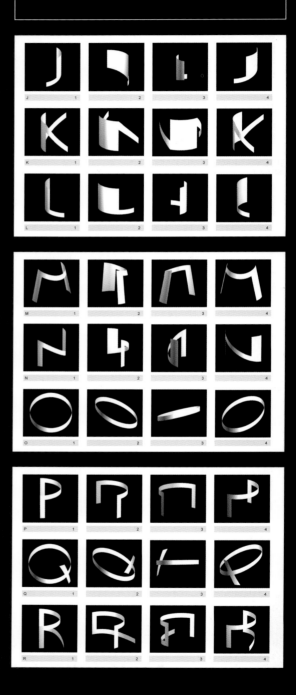

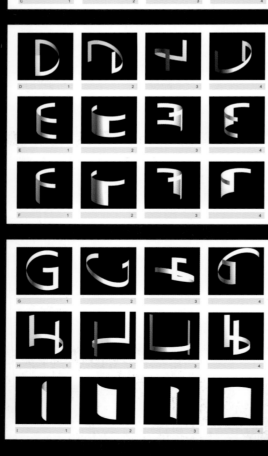

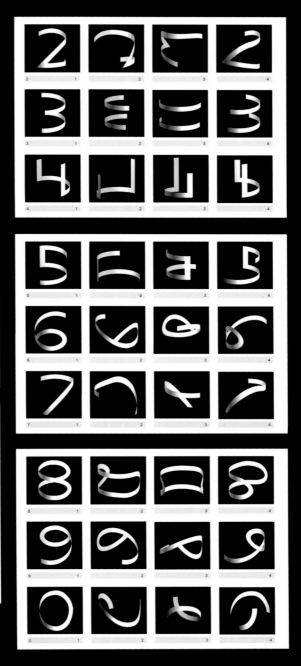

Haltovsky chose a cylinder as the base structure and carved out each letterform from this shape, creating forms that did not have to be designed in three-dimensions, merely cut from a three-dimensional form. When still the letters appear to be paper thin, hence the name Papercut. The outcome is letterforms that are recognizable when viewed from a particular angle, but become abstract formations when viewed from other angles and are fascinating to watch as they again become recognizable.

Starting with this exploration, a new world of three-dimensional letterforms can be created in any language, form, shape and material, and it is suitable for any subject matter or design environment.

Mechanical Organics

Luigi de Aloisio has been pursuing his passion for digital design since 1985 and is also head of the multimedia laboratory of the Accademia di Comunicazione in Milan. Mixing an in-depth knowledge of major software with an artistic background, he creates interactive projects that combine photography, illustration and computer-generated imagery (CGI) with advanced programming. De Aloisio's work takes advantage of the non-linear characteristics of programming languages, while his interest in new creative forms leads him to collaborate on experimental theatre and dance projects.

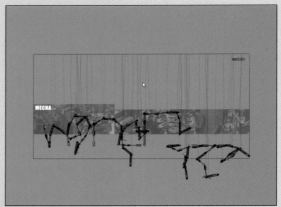

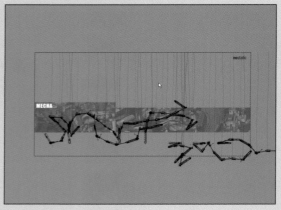

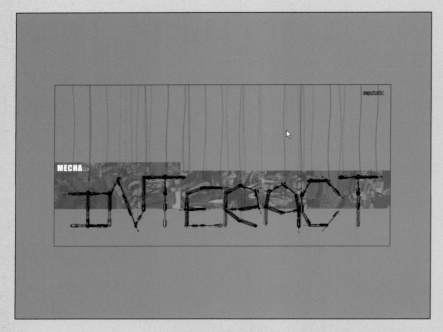

De Aloisio used Macromedia Flash MX and scripts in Action Scripts to create this work. He built an alphabet of mechanical arms with articulated joints. The structure of each arm is determined by the angles between each segment. A series of mechanical arms form the letters of a word.

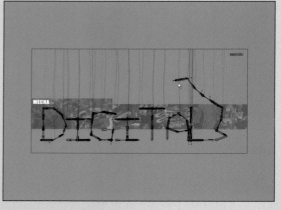

If clicked on, the letters 'dismantle' and chase the mouse. To enable this movement, de Aloisio applied formulas of inverse kinematics to calculate the angles that each segment of the arm must respect.

When the mouse is caught, the arms begin to position themselves in the letters of a new word in the series: MACHINE, FORM, IMAGINE, INTERACT, NOISE, UNIVERSE, MOVE, DIGITAL, EVOLUTION.

TITLE *MECH03* · **FORMAT** DIGITAL INTERACTIVE ANIMATION · **ORIGIN** ITALY ·
DESIGNER, PROGRAMMER LUIGI DE ALOISIO

TITLE *FILAMENTS* · **FORMAT** DIGITAL INTERACTIVE ANIMATION · **ORIGIN**
ITALY · **DESIGNER, PROGRAMMER** LUIGI DE ALOISIO

As the name suggests, this font draws its characters through 'filaments' that evolve on the screen and maintain continuous movement. The filaments have two forms: 'Plastic' and 'Organic'. Plastic type generates its characters from a segment of slightly pliable filament, while Organic creates characters in a painterly gesture with fluid, variable-width filament.

Macromedia Flash MX and Action Script were used to obtain the special motion of the filaments. The characters were drawn by Spline curves because they are soft and capable of being modified by control points. These points are moved by an algorithm that applies a sinusoidal modulation to determine the continuous motion of the curve. Sounds are added to create the right atmosphere.

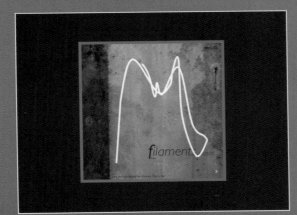

Simulating Nature

De Aloisio produced these studies that simulate the appearance of natural phenomena using text. The outcome is a series of visual, animated interactive poems enriched with sound effects. Moving the mouse initiates the action and controls the phenomena embedded in the text.

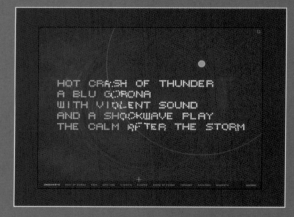

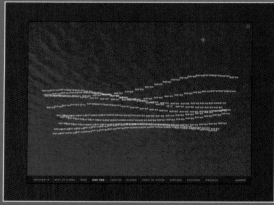

De Aloisio used Macromedia Director and some behaviours in Lingo, to create the effects. Scripts provide the typographic elements while behaviours introduce physical elements, such as inertia, heaviness or shock waves of attraction and repulsion.

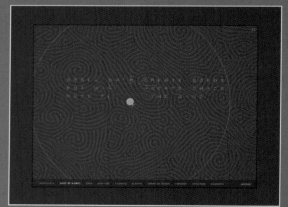

SPECULATING

168 · 169

TITLE *NATURE* · **FORMAT** DIGITAL INTERACTIVE ANIMATION ·
ORIGIN ITALY · **DESIGNER, PROGRAMMER** LUIGI DE ALOISIO

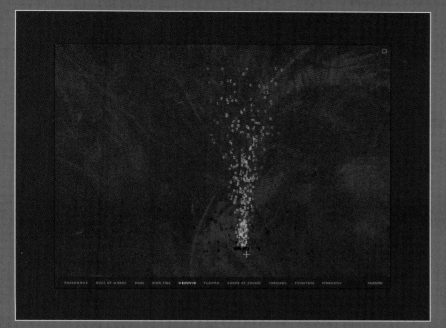

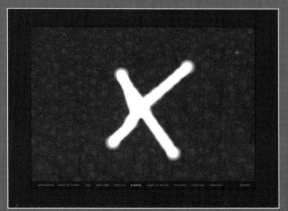

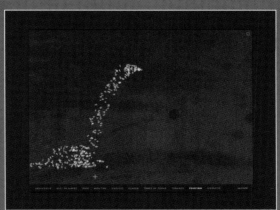

Here, the effects simulate
sand moving in the wind,
rain, a volcano erupting and
a fountain spraying. The
typefaces evolve according to
the direction determined by
the program.

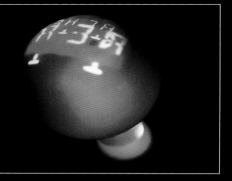

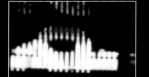

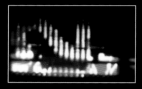

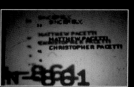

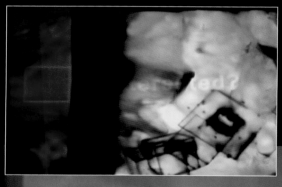

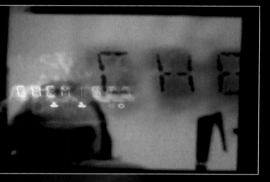

Often relying on optical rather than digital effects, P2 (see p. 16) aims to create a provocative and rich vocabulary that builds on mystery, such as in this collection of visual and typographic studies in motion.

TITLE P2 REEL EXCERPT · **FORMAT** PROMOTIONAL SEQUENCE · **ORIGIN** USA · **DESIGNERS** MATTHEW PACETTI, CHRISTOPHER PACETTI

TITLE THIS WILL FADE · **FORMAT** EXPERIMENTAL SEQUENCE · **ORIGIN** USA · **DESIGNER** MATTHEW PACETTI

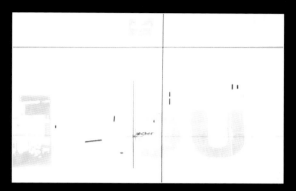

This experimental piece explores transparency and layered type effects. P2 produced a filmic quality from small still-life environments created using objects, video projections and multiple layers of suspended type.

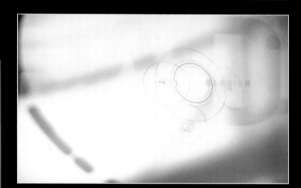

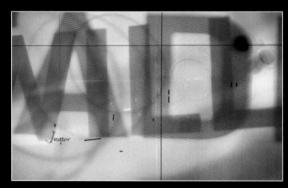

Persian Influence

Iranian graphic designer Reza Abedini has traced a dynamic path during his fifteen-year career. His professional work spans from print to film, with a keen emphasis on Persian type and calligraphy. This short film shows how his graphic-design work depends on Persian art, culture and civilization; it is one of the first examples of Persian typography in motion. Abedini discovered a form that worked in motion while remaining loyal to Persian type and calligraphy.

In Iranian–Islamic culture words are of great importance. Abedini's idea originated from the old religious saying that all the concepts in the world are hidden inside words, and all the words' meanings are found inside one sentence, and the meaning of the sentence can be found in just a word, and finally the word's meaning can be found inside its very first point.

In Abedini's opinion a movie needs a strong and significant beginning followed by the main story and then a meaningful final part, which sometimes relates to the beginning.

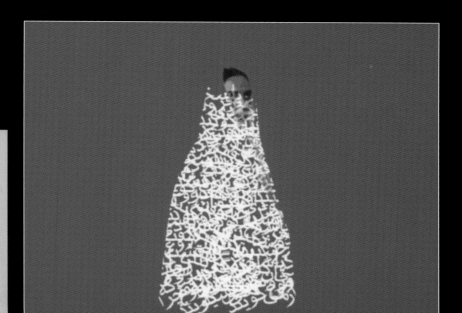

TITLE *IN THE BEGINNING…* · **FORMAT** SHORT VIDEO ·
ORIGIN IRAN · **DIRECTOR, DESIGNER, ANIMATOR**
REZA ALAVI

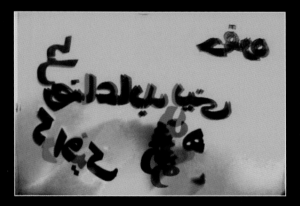

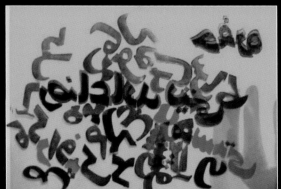

This movie begins with a
single point on screen, and
through that many characters,
words, humans and artworks
are born. The point multiplies
and creates everything.
Finally, all that has been
created contracts and goes
back to the first point.

Alphabet City

Co-author of *Type in Motion: Innovations in Digital Graphics* Jeff Bellantoni has spent a number of years establishing the undergraduate animation and design course at Mercy College in New York. His next venture is to develop the Roy Disney Animation Studio. For him, the most rewarding aspect of a career devoted to art and design education is witnessing the success of his former students in the industry and in academia. Bellantoni also explores the non-commercial side of design in his personal studio.

Bellantoni rescued these aluminium letterforms from the White Plains, NY Parking Garage during its demolition. He reuses them in a number of ways: mounting them on the wall in the hallways at Mercy College, using them as 'models' for paintings and using them to create a physical space.

Tired of the ease with which one can manipulate digital typography – even three-dimensional letterforms – Bellantoni was interested in working within the limitations of material forms. He arranged his found letters into this 'city' and captured hundreds of sequenced images using extreme lighting. He approached photographing this environment as if flying over a cityscape.

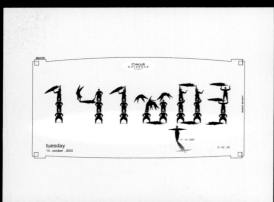

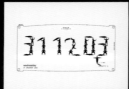

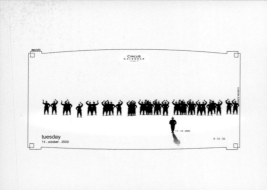

ACKNOWLEDGMENTS

I am indebted to following for their consultation, generous assistance and contributions to the making of this book: every designer and artist who took time out of their busy schedule to collect and submit their work; School of the Arts, Virginia Commonwealth University; Nicole Arreola of Montgomery and Company; Julie Shevach and Danielle James of Trollbäck & Company; Mike Eastwood of EyeballNYC; Steve Kazanjian; Kim Yale of Yale Brand Marketing/ Digital Kitchen; Ben Grube of Digital Kitchen; Leslie Mais of LMPR/FUEL; Vivian Rosenthal of Tronic Studio; Kevin Aratari of mOcean; Clare Matthias of Fitch; Jim Kenney of CCA; Dan Boyarski of CMU; Sandy Wheeler and Roy McKelvey of VCU; Nathalie Fallaha of LAU; George Plesko and Eddie Opara at Yale University; John Stanko; Jeff Bellantoni; Lucas Dietrich, Catherine Hall and Alice Park of Thames & Hudson; and most definitely my friends, colleagues and family. I thank you all.

A group of acrobats perform to music in a circus: they run on to the screen and assemble into numbers that form the date selected by the user. Should the acrobats be disturbed by the mouse passing over or clicking on them, they lose their balance and the numeric pyramids tumble down.

Luigi de Aloisio used Macromedia Flash MX to create his acrobats. He studied a series of possible movements and then rendered these in vectors. Each group of acrobats reads the position they should take inside the selected date and performs an animated loop to create the required number.